A book for the non-specialist music lover
NO musical examples
NO discography
NO free CD

Unheard Melodies

or
Trampolining in the Vatican

Enjoying Music the Grown-up Way

Unheard Melodies

or

Trampolining in the Vatican

Enjoying Music the Grown-up Way

Paul Drayton

ATHENA PRESS
LONDON

Unheard Melodies or
Trampolining in the Vatican
Enjoying Music the Grown-up Way
Copyright © Paul Drayton 2008

ISBN 10-digit: 1 84748 073 X
ISBN 13-digit: 978 1 84748 073 6

First Published 2008 by
ATHENA PRESS
Queen's House, 2 Holly Road
Twickenham TW1 4EG
United Kingdom

Printed for Athena Press

Heard melodies are sweet, but those unheard
Are sweeter; therefore, ye soft pipes, play on;
Not to the sensual ear, but, more endear'd,
Pipe to the spirit ditties of no tone.

John Keats, 1795–1821

I hear singing and there's no one there,
I smell blossoms and the trees are bare.

Irving Berlin, 1888–1989

To anyone who'll listen

Contents

I
Prelude

Strauss and the Air Guitar

There's a story about the composer Richard Strauss. Conducting a rehearsal of one of his own works, he was not satisfied with a certain passage. The part for kettle drums, marked to be played very softly, was never quite soft enough. Several times the passage was repeated and each time the eminent composer indicated that the effect was too loud. It was played yet again and this time, having exhausted his supply of softness, the hapless player fell back on that most dependable of musical resources – total inaudibility. In desperation but with utter conviction, he simply mimed and made no sound at all. The music ended and all eyes turned to Strauss. 'Perfect!' he beamed.

This story is often told with the implication that even the greatest musicians can be caught out. Orchestral players in particular delight in repeating stories that seem to (and sometimes do) discredit their old enemy the conductor. 'Ha ha,' they seem to say, 'we fooled him again.' On the other hand, musicians know that the power to imagine music is almost limitless. That ultra-soft drum note was real enough to Strauss. And musicians will sometimes tell you that their best performances are the imagined ones, inside their own heads. Wasn't there a *Desert Island Discs* castaway on the radio – a distinguished pianist, I recall – who put his cards on the table right from the start? He was not too bothered about recordings. Given the choice, he would far rather take eight musical scores to the fictional desert island. There he could read them through and intuit each piece of music in his own private and faultless interpretation.

For every listener who nodded sympathetically (musicians themselves, perhaps), I would guess there were countless others who would have welcomed the opportunity to strangle him. Such pretentiousness – and on BBC Radio 4, too! But silent perform-ances can be a blessing. Take the aspiring teenage rock-god. To suffering parents, a manic guitar-solo on an unamplified tennis-racquet may be a welcome alternative to the real thing. When a middle-aged husband attempts to recapture his lost youth with flailing power-chords on the air guitar, his wife suffers only embarrassment and not deafness. Miraculously, the skull of the performer has enlarged to the size of Wembley arena, and the sound inside it is thrilling a capacity crowd, but no collateral damage is done.

Strauss, an experienced conductor and composer, was familiar enough with the sound he had written to be able to imagine it. Our latter-day air guitarist probably drank in the music he admires with his mother's milk and has no trouble recreating the sound mentally. But what about music that has never been heard by any living person?

In contemplating that famous Grecian urn, the poet Keats, intrigued by the painted figures piping soundlessly away, struggled to envisage this music of a vanished world. What might these sounds have been like? he wondered. Fascinated by the unknowable nature of such music – its awesome remoteness and mystery – he felt there must be something especially potent about these ditties of no tone, which were frozen in time and could only have their melodies guessed at. We can never bridge that gap of two thousand years or more, but, somehow, even to try is worthwhile and inspiring. These unheard melodies are in a strange way superior to the real thing.

But we may say all this is poetic fancy. In the real world what could be better or simpler than the experience of hearing music in an actual performance? Well, of course this is fine in one sense, but there is so much more we can learn. Music is a bit like plywood; our experience of even the most familiar work may just be a veneer hiding a multitude of laminations, elements that our ears, and sometimes even the ears of a trained musician, are unable to grasp, even when we know those elements are there. And laminations, as any DIY enthusiast may tell you, mean strength.

That is really the theme of this book.

Anyone can hear music as a pleasant and soothing background. 'Improve your mood with Classic FM,' we are repeatedly told. Some of us may choose to listen more attentively, perhaps, to the lunchtime recital on BBC Radio 3. But even this merely scratches the surface.

As the acerbic conductor Sir Thomas Beecham is supposed to have remarked, 'The English don't really like music – they just like the noise it makes.' Well, noise – or sound, to give it a more respectful name – is a good place to start, but it's only the end product of a much greater construct. One of the greatest joys of music is not what we hear, but what we know. Keats's heard melodies are sweet enough, but they comprise only a fraction of the musical iceberg. An examination of the hidden portion will reveal some astonishing secrets.

'Had I Three Ears I'd Hear Thee'
– Macbeth, IV.i

When we hear a new piece of music, how much detail can our ears really pick up? Clearly a lot depends on the skill and experience of the listener. Let's imagine then that you are motivated and receptive, but with no special musical training. Let's assume too that your situation is conducive to concentrated listening – perhaps a quiet room, with no yelling kids or roaring traffic. Then into that room comes the sound of music. For the sake of simplicity let's make it the tune *Greensleeves*.

If it's being played live on the tuba, by your diminutive son preparing for his Grade I exam, a whole range of complicating reactions might arise. Bless him! He's almost hidden by the enormous instrument. The tone may be a bit rough, but hasn't he improved since he started going to Miss Blaster for lessons? I do wish he'd clean those awful trainers, though... etc.

So let's make things more impersonal. The music comes to you from good speakers, played from a CD of a professional musician, whose identity you neither know nor care about. And forget the tuba. It's going to be a flute. A single, unaccompanied flute. And there will be no singing of the *Greensleeves* words, which would add a far too specific message. One other thing. You almost certainly know the tune. In fact, you can already hear it playing in your head, can't you? But let's pretend you are hearing it for the first time. What's your reaction? And I don't mean, 'That's rather pretty, isn't it?' Subjective, emotional responses are banned for the purpose of this exercise. It is the music itself that interests us. What purely technical and objective information do your ears gather as the music plays? Just take a moment to close your eyes and listen...

Perhaps you hear the prevailing rhythm first, the short-long-short-long pattern that gives the tune its lilting quality. Then, as you hear more, you might sense the arching shape of the phrases – a few notes that climb up, then a few that drop down, then a similar pattern over again. You may notice that the first half consists of two phrases which are the same – or nearly the same, since the second one turns around at the end in order to sound 'finished off'. The second half begins strikingly, with a sudden much higher note from which the subsequent notes drop down quite a long way. That too is repeated, except that the same little twist is added to finish things off.

All of this has happened in a space of about forty seconds, assuming a comfortably average tempo. And those forty seconds have fallen quite audibly into four distinct sections of about ten seconds each, all of which relate to one another in some way. So, this very old and disarmingly simple tune (often attributed to Henry VIII, but more correctly acknowledged as anonymous) has a fairly sophisticated internal structure, which reveals itself to the attentive listener over a time span little more than that of a TV commercial. With so much information for the brain to process in one brief melody, what happens if we consider works by composers who delight in making things complicated?

Well, let's take it one step at a time.

Suppose we add a second instrument, an oboe, say, playing another line designed to fit with the *Greensleeves* tune. What we hear of that line depends on how much attention it demands from us. If it consists of just a few long sustained notes, we will merely register its presence and perhaps enjoy the way in which it fits snugly with the tune. If, however, the added line is busy with quick flurries of notes, we may find it drawing our ears away from the flute's tune. Like a hyperactive child in a playgroup, it seeks our attention. The finale of *St Paul's Suite* by Holst is a case in point.

If we add a third line, a bassoon, say, we may be even more uncertain as to where to direct our attention. Unlike our limbs, our ears do not function independently, but work as a team. When faced with a number of simultaneous melodic lines, they scan them rapidly for little sonic events that disturb the flow; rather like a sheepdog, darting instinctively this way and that, to round up the odd sheep with a will of its own. A trained musician

– even one with three ears! – could not pay equal heed to all three lines. Some sort of sifting process must take place.

If the *Greensleeves* tune is played as the highest of the three lines in terms of pitch, the human ear will probably register it as the most important of the three. But the situation may be flexible and we need to monitor it constantly. There may be some demanding element of independence, or hyperactivity, or perhaps of differing loudness, which confuses the issue and diverts our attention to new areas.

Sometimes the tune may be the lowest line of the three, acting as a bass part. Pitched at this low level, below the other parts, we are less likely to follow it, and if, as sometimes happens, it is hiding in the middle, even an attentive listener may fail to spot it. The filling in a musical sandwich declares its presence much less readily than its culinary equivalent. And, of course, there may be far more than three layers.

So far we have thought about individual musical lines progressing from note to note in a 'horizontal' plane, like three people speaking at once. It may be that if the human race is exposed for long enough to *The Jerry Springer Show*, it will develop a heightened capacity for understanding three people talking, or shouting, at once. Perhaps in due course dwellers in the noisy, modern world will evolve by natural selection into multi-linear listeners. Meanwhile even the best-regulated of families could give us some practice:

Mother:	I've told you before – no skateboarding till you've finished your homework.
Father:	Oh, for God's sake. I only clicked on this and it deleted the whole bloody file.
TV:	The news at six o'clock. The Prime Minister was today abducted by aliens.

To make sense of three people speaking at once is hard enough, but in music there is a different kind of information overload. Admittedly, it's not the literal information conveyed by words, but each line has its own musical sense, a shape and coherence planned by the composer. And at any given moment, there are three separate notes being played, making chords. This 'vertical' harmonic aspect is vying for our attention along with the horizontal one, but to follow the subtle shifts in this vertical sound, and the individual progress of the three instruments, is well nigh on impossible. Even the most musically gifted of listeners may find their ears defaulting to a more passive, non-analytical response. 'Advanced Level Music Aural Perception' mode gives way to the 'Let it wash pleasantly over you' approach.

This approach is not unlike viewing a painted portrait with half-closed eyes, smoothing over the individual brush-strokes, or maybe taking a step back and allowing your brain to mix jangling greens, yellows and purples into tones appropriate to the human complexion. Then you may wish, at your leisure, to peer more closely, guidebook in hand, to scrutinise the artist's handiwork.

Music, unfortunately, is not so obliging. It moves too fast. What is more, musical notation is not accessible to everyone. Paintings deliver themselves directly to the eye. Musical notation requires a practised intermediary to breathe life into it.

So, how and when did melodies begin to be combined? In mediaeval times, the idea was in its infancy. Composers were often attached to a church, cathedral or monastery, and the sound of single-lined or monophonic plainchant ran in their blood-stream. To blend other parts with these ancient chants was a tempting challenge. One obvious solution was to add a similar line of melody running parallel to the tune; think railway lines, which may curve and change direction, but are always the same distance from each other.

But if the two sung parts were to move together in a con-trolled manner, notes must have definite metric values. A regular reference point was also needed. This was the *tactus*, or what we would call a beat. With a regular pulse beating at the heart of the music, a few judicious decorations could be introduced without disturbing the correct correlation of the voices. From time immemorial, the sinuously beautiful plainchant melodies had held sway in churches all over Europe, unaccompanied and with only the subtlest fluctuations of rhythm. Now they were being clothed in a rhythmic straitjacket, and their venerable solitude was at an end. They entered into a musical partnership.

It's for their own good, cutting-edge mediaeval composers insisted. Polyphony is the sound of the future. And if two parallel melodic lines could be sung together, why not three?

So with the original tune, the bourdon, allocated either to the middle or to the uppermost voice, two extra parts were now added. Since each additional voice-part created a new 'false' melody, the style became known as fauxbourdon.

Some of the most celebrated exponents of this three-layered technique were a group of fourteenth-century English – yes, English – musicians, known to us as the School of Worcester. They are not identifiable as individuals, but the Worcester sound made waves across Europe. Their work is now preserved in the archive known as the Old Worcester Source (all right, I made that last bit up).

Crabs and Canals

Composers, always ready to push the envelope in matters of complexity, lost no time in giving each vocal part much greater freedom in shape and rhythm. The two-part railway-line effect had expanded to three parts, still moving largely in parallel motion; think telegraph wires as seen from a moving train. But this soon evolved into what we might call the 'spaghetti effect'. Each melodic line moved freely, and with apparent randomness in relation to the others. But 'apparent' is the key word here. In reality, the relationships might be very precise and very mathematical. It's just that you can't hear them.

At the simplest level, a musical note has two properties: pitch (how high or low it is) and duration (how long or short it is). It follows, then, that any melody, consisting of a string of notes, can be sung, or played, either forwards or backwards. If we start at the last note and work, in written terms, from right to left, we will end up with a reversed version of the original melody. This is usually described as retrograde motion. Retrograde derives from the Latin for 'backwards step'. Another way of describing this process was *cancrizans*, or crab-like.

Strictly speaking, crabs move sideways rather than backwards, but perhaps we should think of the tune scuttling across the paper, sideways, from left to right and then back again from right to left. Or perhaps we should just not worry too much about it.

The same process, using letters of the alphabet, is a more familiar trick. Its official name, palindrome, comes from the Greek for 'running back again' (though why we should now be running rather than stepping is not clear). There are several well-known palindromes, such as 'Madam, I'm Adam', a polite introduction in the Garden of Eden, or 'Able was I 'ere I saw Elba', unconvincing in the mouth of anyone except perhaps Napoleon...

The sense here is strictly subservient to the charm of the puzzle. Here's a longer one, which makes its job easier by using only one vowel: 'A Man, A Plan, A Canal, Panama'.

Laconic, but meaningful in a rather pleasing way, isn't it? Anyone hearing that phrase for the first time may not suspect anything odd about it, and will probably reach for a pen and paper to verify its palindromic property. A musical palindrome, or retrograde, is even harder to verify by hearing alone, and needs to be worked out on paper even if it's only a few notes long. In fact, some musical retrogrades are protracted to an alarming degree. A good retrograde should make reasonable musical sense in both directions. And if it does, imagine the composer's smug satisfaction!

Suppose, then, that a certain piece has three independent melodic lines. The top line contains about 130 notes of various durations and pitches. The middle line has exactly the same notes in reverse order – a *cancrizans* version of the upper line. The two lines are sung together and fit perfectly. Imagine the odds against that! Careful planning would be vital.

But what about the lowest line of our piece? Not to be outdone, it proceeds in such a way that the second half of the tune is a *cancrizans* version of the first half. In other words, having reached the halfway point it unwinds itself in the opposite direction. It is symmetrical around its central note just as the Panama palindrome is symmetrical around the letter 'C'. And all the time it is designed to fit harmonically with the upper two voices as they perform their own mathematical convolutions. The whole thing looking something like this:

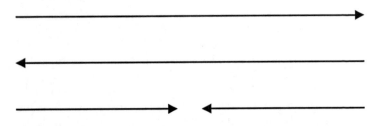

Am I making all this up? By no means. And far from being the brainchild of some anally-retentive composer of the twentieth century, precisely such a piece was written in about 1360 by

Guillaume de Machaut (whose surname is pronounced not unlike 'cashew'). This is seriously early – the birth of Mozart lay 400 years in the future.

Why did he write it? Well, the sung text gives us a clue: '*Ma fin est mon commencement et mon commencement ma fin*'. It may not trip off the tongue but we get the point: 'My end is my beginning and my beginning my end'. And to add to the fun he adopts the regular mediaeval practice of writing out only a skeleton score of the basic material, so that by following his instructions we can supply the missing bits. What we have here is a mediaeval, flat-pack music kit to be assembled by the customer.

I would like to have known this French contemporary of Chaucer. He was a priest, poet, composer and keen traveller. Best known for his polyphonic setting of the mass, probably the earliest ever written, he also turned out quite racy love-songs. Whoever said mediaeval music is dull?

In terms of theoretical skills, mediaeval composers were no slouches and matching the music to the text in some abstract way was not uncommon. But why go to such extremes? A strong motivation must have been the shamelessly self-indulgent, back-patting, grinning-from-ear-to-ear pleasure of making it all fit. And once we, as bystanders, are in on the act, how very contagious is that pleasure!

And this glorious self-indulgence did not end with the Middle Ages. It is what composers have always done. How wonderful to discover, as we listen to a 1949 string octet by Darius Milhaud – pronounced as in '*O sole mio*', more or less – that what we are hearing is an amalgam of two distinct string quartets (nos. 14 and 15), cunningly constructed so as to be playable separately or together. Contrapuntal ingenuity of such staggering pointlessness deserves our admiration.

Then there is the case of the reversible minuet. Like many eighteenth-century composers, Haydn churned out minuets like they were going out of fashion – which indeed they were. But there's one particular harpsichord minuet labelled *Al Rovescio* which shows a real sense of mischief. The second half, ten bars long, is the first half in reverse: rhythm, pitches, harmony, everything! Each half is repeated, giving the music time to sink in, and then comes the trio. This is also in two halves, each repeated, and once again the second is an exact reversal of the first. Finally, the minuet is played again. This always happens. '*Da Capo*', the composer tells us; 'from the top', saving himself the trouble of writing it all out again. But this time, if there were any justice, the final playing would be drowned out by a standing ovation for Haydn. Not great music, but a great musical party-trick.

On an altogether more sublime level is the Act I finale of Mozart's 1787 opera, *Don Giovanni*. We are at a sumptuous party where dancing is about to begin. Three ensembles strike up three different dance-tunes in three different rhythms. This would have been meat and drink to the twentieth-century American composer Charles Ives, who relished the cacophony of three marching bands thumping out a variety of tunes at the same time. As a child in Danbury, Connecticut, he had been fascinated by this kind of accidental musical chaos on festival days, and had later incorporated it into his orchestral works, where conflicting rhythms, tempos and harmonies jostle together in an exhilarating racket. There was no pretence of trying to fit things together. None of the art that conceals art. This was music in the raw, and calculated confusion reigned.

But Mozart was a creature of the Enlightenment, where things must fit, and order, not instinct, is the hallmark of art. Or, to put it in the mythological terms of ancient Greece, light-loving Apollo, not fun-loving Dionysus, rules. So, as the three bands at Don Giovanni's party launch into their respective dances, the composer's skill is tested to destruction. The score indicates three slow beats for a minuet, three quick beats for a waltz, and two for a quadrille, all at the same time. The bands strike up, one by one, and before entering the fray each one draws its bows across pairs of open strings as if tuning up, not randomly, but in strict accordance with Mozart's instructions. Finally, everyone is playing three quite disparate pieces, not to mention the singing of the characters in the opera. Musical bars stagger drunkenly across the pages of the score. Anarchy threatens; but what do we actually hear? Miraculously, of course, for this is Mozart, everything fits like Lego, so perfectly that you can be sure most of the audience would be oblivious to the conjuring trick being pulled off in front of their very ears. No wonder Don Giovanni sings, '*Va bene in verita!*' It's really going well, isn't it?

But wait, for from the cold corridors of correctness comes a wailing and a gnashing of teeth. Does this not all reek of exclusivity?

First there was Machaut, with his vocal cryptogram. His music is pleasant enough in a quirky, mediaeval sort of way, but below the deceptively simple surface there is all manner of smart-alecky cleverness going on, of which we know nothing. And even when we do know about it, we can't hear it anyway!

Four hundred years later, composers were still at it. Playing games with us and laughing up their satin-embroidered sleeves. Mozart, though far from being the giggling buffoon shown in the film *Amadeus*, must have winked triumphantly at his players as they negotiated these peculiar challenges. And behind him the powdered and periwigged audience chattered on in blissful ignorance.

So, are we talking ego-trips here? Private jokes? In a way, yes, but this is more than mere artistic vanity. The sound has become one component in a sort of mind game or puzzle, and to appreciate these seemingly unremarkable musical moments, one needs privileged information. So for the average, run-of-the-mill listener, doesn't it look like a blatant case of – murmur it softly – elitism? Perhaps, but you're in on the secret now, so just sit back and savour that elitism. Mmm!

Phantom Bar Codes

Here is a little experiment to while away a few minutes on a rainy afternoon. All you need is a piano. The better in tune it is, the better the result will be (a Steinway grand piano is preferred, but not essential!).

Find the low C two octaves below middle C. I'm sure you know that middle C is the one nearest the keyhole – the keyhole of the piano, that is! Now with your left hand press this low C very slowly and carefully, so as to not to make any sound. Keep it held firmly down, then with your right hand locate a chord of C major (C+E+G) in the octave above your silent note. When you're sure you have the correct three notes lined up, strike the chord as loudly and sharply as you can. Don't hold it down, but strike as many times as you wish, the object being to create as much noise as possible. You can even get bystanders to sing and shout and clap their hands inside the piano to add to the general tumult. Finish your noisy chord-playing and listen! What do you hear?

What you should hear is a ghostly chord of C, a cluster of notes spread out higher in pitch than the one low C you are holding down. Depending on the quality and size of your piano, and a bit on the acuity of your hearing, you should be aware of a sort of sonic rainbow, comprising perhaps half a dozen phantom frequencies all contained within that one low note.

With your finger still holding it down, the low C is the only note capable of making a sound. All the dampers on the rest of the piano are touching their strings, muting them, except for the one attached to your vibrating low C. Now let go of it. What do you hear? Silence. Which proves that the phantom chord was in fact being produced by a single string.

In the 1660s, Isaac Newton performed a famous experiment. By directing sunlight into a prism in a darkened room, he showed that so-called white light is in fact made up of a range, or spectrum, of different colours. For countless generations people must have gazed in wonder as a rainbow hung miraculously in a stormy sky or in a sunlit waterfall, but it took a seventeenth-century English scientist to discover the underlying nature of light. Sound too can be broken down into its constituent parts, but this similar property was spotted very much earlier by the Greek philosopher, mathematician and musician Pythagoras, about 500 years before the birth of Christ.

Generations of schoolchildren, who knew only of his unhealthy interest in right-angled triangles, might have warmed to Pythagoras had they known how much time he spent twanging a sort of single-stringed zither, or monochord. His experiments taught him the jaw-dropping fact that a stretched string vibrates not only throughout its whole length, but also in two halves, three thirds, four quarters and so on. All at the same time! These variously vibrating portions of string combine to produce a spectral halo of faint notes, which sound above the main note, or fundamental. This family of overtones, or upper partials, is known as the harmonic series, and it is their ghostly presence that gives the fundamental note its special tone-quality.

The column of air inside a wind instrument operates in a similar way. The complete vibrating column of air creates the fundamental note, while the vibrating subdivisions of this column add overtones to give the note its characteristic timbre. Even when playing an identical note, a trumpet, or a violin, or a clarinet, will sound different because the relative strengths of its overtones vary. Like a supermarket barcode, every musical instrument has its own individual profile of harmonics.

In an electronic music-studio, the harmonic series can be artificially manipulated to produce the sound of a virtual trumpet, or oboe, or whatever you choose. With all the natural harmonics removed, what remains can be somewhat bland and hollow in comparison, a little like the sound of the recorder. Now, I enjoy a well-played recorder as much as the next person, but its tone does have a certain naked and vulnerable quality. And now we see why. That simple but venerable instrument has almost no overtones to hide its modesty, and therefore comes close to the pure but rather characterless sound that physicists can measure as a sine wave.

Only the tuning fork rivals it in this respect, though sadly Vivaldi, who wrote prolifically for the recorder, never wrote a concerto for tuning fork. As far as we know…

One or two instruments do the reverse. When a sustained fundamental note is played, our attention is drawn mainly to the cloud of harmonics, whose 'changes of colour' are manipulated by the player. The Jew's harp does this through the player changing the shape of the mouth. The didgeridoo does a similar thing, blowing rather than twanging. And it has even sneaked into the orchestra. Look out for *Earth Cry* by the Australian composer Peter Sculthorpe.

Pythagoras, with his passion for numbers and proportions, must have been delighted to discover that the overtones of any given note rise in a satisfying mathematical pattern. Let's return to that low C played on a piano. When you press the key, it is the low C itself, the fundamental, that we are conscious of hearing as the real pitch of the note. This is produced by the string vibrating over its complete length.

But, like every other note on the keyboard, this low C is nourished by a range of higher tones of which we can be blissfully unaware. The first and strongest overtone will sound the C an octave higher, a paler twin of the principal note, created by the string vibrating in two halves:

Fundamental

XzzzzzzzzzzzzzzzzzzzzzzzzzzzzzzzzzzzzzzzzzzzzzzzzzzzzzzzzzzzzX

Overtone 1

XzzzzzzzzzzzzzzzzzzzzzzzzzzzzOzzzzzzzzzzzzzzzzzzzzzzzzzzzzX

Now, moving on from this higher C, step up the keyboard, via D–E–F, to G. We are now twelve (inclusive) white-note steps from the original low C. This G is the pitch of the next overtone, caused by the vibration of the string in three equal portions.

Overtone 2

XzzzzzzzzzzzzzzzzzOzzzzzzzzzzzzzzzzzzOzzzzzzzzzzzzzzzzzX

Then comes the C above that, from the string vibrating in quarters, followed by the E, caused by the string vibrating in fifths.

Overtone 3

XzzzzzzzzzzzzzzOzzzzzzzzzzzzzzOzzzzzzzzzzzzzzOzzzzzzzzzzzzzzX

Overtone 4

XzzzzzzzzzzOzzzzzzzzzzOzzzzzzzzzzOxxxxxxxxxxOxxxxxxxxxxX

And there are more beyond that, crowding ever closer together, becoming weaker in volume, but all contributing to the tonal ripeness of the fundamental note – rather like the bouquet of a fine wine, I've no doubt. Take them all away and we're talking *vin ordinaire*.

God's Hymn Sheet

Organists, and particularly organ builders, know all about overtones. The mixture, or mutation, stops of an organ call into play special ranks of pipes designed to add extra overtones to the regular notes. They have exotic names like *quintaton* and *sesquialtera*, should you be interested. Adding in extra overtones is meat and drink to organists, and sometimes they get carried away with their own ingenuity. How often have the discerning members of a church congregation (there are some) listened in horror as the melody of a Bach Chorale Prelude is soloed out in what sounds like the wrong key, a fifth higher than the surrounding musical landscape? This is the infamous *quintaton* stop, which makes the second overtone stronger than the fundamental.

Organists seem to take a perverse delight in such migraine-inducing effects. In fact, the organ itself is not to everyone's taste. Strolling in a country churchyard with a friend, Sir Thomas Beecham, the orchestral conductor, is said to have come across a headstone inscribed, 'Sacred to the memory of a fine organist and a wonderful musician'.

'Odd they should put them both in the same grave,' the conductor is said to have snorted to his companion.

While dissociating myself entirely from this implied calumny, I believe that a sensitive soul might be scarred for life by exposure to the *quintaton* stop. And if Sir Thomas Beecham really had delivered all the acerbic remarks attributed to him, he would have had to start in the cradle and live to be 120!

To be fair, organ builders have over centuries added significantly to our knowledge of the way musical tones behave, and have used that knowledge to their advantage. If, for instance, two different notes are played together, their combined frequencies will produce a new higher note – a summation tone – while the difference between their two frequencies will also create a new lower note – a differential, or resultant, tone. These are hard to hear, but in theory, at least, we get four notes for the price of two.

This phenomenon can be handy in a church where space is limited. Rather than trying to install the thirty-two-foot pipes needed to generate really deep notes, an organ builder can utilise two pipes of more manageable size. With one pipe delivering a low C and a shorter one delivering the G a fifth higher, then by skilfully suppressing the unwanted summation tone, a phantom, super-deep C can be coaxed out of thin air. Taking a frequency, measured in cycles per second, or hertz, at random:

50 Hz added to 75 Hz = 125 Hz (summation tone).

50 Hz subtracted from 75 Hz = 25 Hz (differential tone).

The gruff-voiced offspring of this relationship is a rather weakly specimen, but worth having if there is no alternative.

When measuring gaps, or intervals, between pitches, or frequencies, white-note steps on the piano are a pretty blunt instrument to use as counting units. Totting up adjacent notes, or semitones, disregarding whether they are black or white, gets us a bit further.

To explain this, imagine our fundamental low C represents someone living at ground-level (floor 0) in a very high tower block. Then the first overtone lives on the twelfth floor, the second overtone on the nineteenth, the third on the twenty-fourth, the next on the twenty-eighth floor, the next on the thirty-first, and so on.

It's a hot day, so all the windows are open. Standing outside in the street we can hear the fundamental tenant easily. The others, though, sing their notes more remotely.

Admittedly, this analogy begins to break down as we would find some higher overtones showing an odd preference for living beneath the floorboards. But it gets us started with a whole-number sequence of 12–19–24–28–31... Enough analogies for the time being – and apologies to those with an analogy allergy.

Even the semitones we have just been counting are pretty slippery customers, with a hazy definition, as we shall see. Counting vibrations per second, Hz, is much more precise. Each note vibrates at a certain rate depending on its pitch. The higher the pitch, the faster the vibration. In modern concert-pitch, the A three semitones below middle C should vibrate at 220 Hz. Its first overtone, sounding the A an octave higher, will register at 440 Hz. This is the pitch of an oboe A, against which most orchestras check their tuning. Above this the series continues with E (660 Hz), A (880 Hz), C# (1,100 Hz), E (1,320 Hz) and so on. The gap in terms of vibration stays constant (220 Hz), but as the pitch rises the overtones become closer, in a regular arithmetical progression.

We find a similar process in many aspects of the natural world. A tree, for example, with its system of branches and twigs diminishing in size as they grow outwards from the trunk; a river system on a map bifurcating into narrower tributaries and streams. The same goes for arteries and smaller blood vessels, or ripples in a pond, spreading out in wider, weaker circles. All these processes can be described mathematically, as Pythagoras suspected.

To stand in a vast Gothic cathedral and sing plainchant must be to feel part of some greater natural process. A thousand years ago sharp-eared monks must have picked up the ghostly second overtone, 'singing along' with their unison male voices. There is even a theory that it was this mysterious parallel sound, the sound of the building itself, which gave rise to the mediaeval organum, or plainchant sung in parallel fifths. It made perfect sense for a few higher-voiced monks to duplicate the strongest natural musical overtone of the building.

But there was a glitch which had exercised the mind of Pythagoras, and still casts a shadow over the perfection of the harmonic series. Compare the frequencies of two notes a fifth apart (E above A, or G above C, for example). The ratio of frequencies will be 3:2. If the A sounds at 220 Hz, the E above it will sound at 330 Hz, half as much again. This is not so much music as physics. It's the way things are.

And this is the glitch. If we keep going, building fifth upon fifth at an exact ratio of 3:2, the resulting chain arrives after twelve links at a frequency which is very nearly a multiple of the one you started with. Very nearly but not quite. If you started with a low C you end up extremely close to a C seven octaves higher. It's a bit like laying slabs around a circular pond and having to cut an inch off the final slab to make it fit.

Take this rising chain of pure fifths: C-G-D-A-E-B-F#-C#-G#-D#-A#-E#-B#.

It looks all right. We've arrived at B# (B sharp), which is the same as C, isn't it? Well, yes, on a keyboard it is. But that's because a piano, if properly tuned, is tuned flat! Those advanced instrumentalists who minutely adjust their pitch as they go – string players, singers, and others – don't always quite agree with the tuning of pianos. When they're being accompanied by one, they compromise – they have to. But a string quartet, for example, unsullied by the presence of a piano, will often play with purer pitch intervals between their notes.

So how big is the discrepancy between C and B#? Well, it's small – less than a semitone – but more than enough to interest the old theorists. In honour of the Greek mastermind, they called it the Pythagorean Comma. And in an earlier, more spiritual age it was troubling. Could it be that God was not singing from the same hymn sheet as the human race? Was our music a blurred photocopy of the real thing?

And what should be done to make keyboards sound acceptable in all keys? If you were to keep perfect, or untempered, fifths almost to the end of the chain and then flatten, or temper, the last one to make things right, certain common chords would be perfectly in tune, while others would give a sensation akin to sucking lemons.

A good solution is to distribute the error – the Pythagorean Comma – evenly around all twelve fifths, thus ironing it out. This sensible compromise is known as 'equal temperament'. Using this system, a keyboard player can show off by performing J S Bach's *48 Preludes and Fugues (The Well-tempered Clavier)* in every major and minor key, without the audience squirming in discomfort.

Bach's title draws our attention to the 'well-tempered' property of the keyboard. But he doesn't explain if this means 'equally tempered'. Or does he? An American musicologist has claimed that the answer is there on the title page for all to see, in the form of a coded pattern of squiggles. The fifths are strung out like pegs on a clothes line, and between them tiny kinks show how the twelve equal parts of the Pythagorean comma are to be distributed. One twelfth here, two here, none here, and so on, making the well-tempered system of the title.

The dispute rumbles on. We may never know the answer. And

what a strangely comforting thought that is! A masterpiece played, admired and analysed for nearly 300 years still hangs on to some of its secrets.

Angels and Blue Thunder

Pythagoras and his followers promoted numbers to a godlike status. In a violent and mutable world, it seemed to him that only numbers could be relied upon to behave themselves in an orderly fashion. But they were much more than just a comforting abstraction for philosophers. Pythagoreans saw numbers as the pervading force behind the whole physical universe. The planets themselves moved according to fixed, arithmetical proportions. And since music was numbers made audible, it stood to reason that as the heavenly bodies moved they too made music.

This idea clung on. Even as late as the seventeenth century, the Pythagorean view had its supporters. Astronomers like Johannes Kepler were attracted by the notion of singing planets. This music of the spheres was nothing we could actually hear, of course; it was much too pure for our sullied ears. But maybe we could hear it one day, when we joined the choir invisible…

Shakespeare put the idea into the mouth of Lorenzo in *The Merchant of Venice*, his words later set by Vaughan Williams in the *Serenade to Music*:

> There's not the smallest orb which thou behold'st
> But in his motion like an angel sings,
> Still quiring to the young-eyed cherubims.
> Such harmony is in immortal souls
> But while this muddy vesture of decay
> Doth grossly close us in, we cannot hear it.

Composing music is a mysterious process, even to a composer. Some have invoked the ancient idea of a celestial harmony to explain how music arrives apparently unbidden in the mind. Inspiration, 'breathing in', has long been regarded as a prerequisite of high-quality artistic creation. Composers 'breathe in' some faint echo of the heavenly music. Old music dictionaries used to include an engraving of Handel composing his oratorio *Messiah*, in which the great man half-reclined amid clouds and angels, with a transported look on his rather chubby face. 'Come down and startle composing mortals with immortal fire', implored the poet W H Auden, addressing the patron saint of music, St Cecilia. For Robert Graves, it was The White Goddess, who startled poets into action. Even today, many people, perhaps not creative in themselves, seem to cling to the vague notion of some kind of muse standing sympathetically at the elbow of the creative artist.

Some lucky composers have indeed found that music can emerge with such spontaneity as to seem outside their control. There is always the hard, technical business of sorting ideas out into a musical score, but where do the ideas come from in the first place?

Debussy thought of himself as a vessel through which pre-existent music passed. Using his special skills and heightened sensitivity he could channel music in the same way a radio receiver makes invisible waves perceptible to the human ear. Stravinsky said something similar about his *Rite of Spring*. It was not forged in his brain, but filtered through it. The English composer Cyril Scott typically went further. In his 1958 book *Music – Its Secret Influence Throughout the Ages*, he posited a whole pantheon of spirits, sages, adepts and higher powers continually monitoring the creative output of humanity.

Composers can be the most practical of people when it comes to putting marks on paper, but are inclined to babble mystically when asked to rationalise their craft. Fair enough. After all, it's never a bad idea to stir up a little esoteric fog around your chosen profession.

One foggy mystery that is aired from time to time is the question of colour. A number of composers – and not just composers – claim to hear in colour. Not in a vaguely metaphorical way as in this piece is dark and threatening, or this piece has a rich golden glow. No, this is literal, and though the colours may vary between individuals, the colour-coded composer finds his own experience consistent. The most celebrated example of recent years was the French organist-composer, Olivier Messiaen, who died in 1992. He was astonishingly precise about the hues of his own music, and often wrote the information into his scores. A chord might be orange or pale green, another rose-pink with purple edges.

Schönberg, the original proponent in the 1920s of the serial, or twelve-note, method of composition, had similar colour-linked experiences, as did his friend Kandinsky, a pioneer of abstraction in painting. For Kandinsky the process worked in reverse. He wrote vividly of his response to a sunset in Moscow. 'The city resounded like the *fff* of a giant orchestra. Pink, lilac, yellow, white, blue, pistachio green, flame-red houses, churches each an independent song. The garish green of the grass, the deeper tremolo of the trees, the singing snow with its thousand voices, the allegretto of the bare branches.'

It's been suggested that the Dutch painter, Van Gogh, was also a sufferer (if that is the word) of the condition known as synaesthesia (that *is* the word). Certainly those whirling, starry skies he painted seem on the point of fizzing into audible life. But there's no discernible logic in all of this. Each case is different. A neurologist of my acquaintance had a patient for whom thunder was blue. It wasn't that thunder merely evoked the idea of blue. The sound of thunder and the concept of blueness were inseparably linked. Thunder sounded blue in the way grass looks green. It seems that in the brain of people with this condition, there is a kind of synaptic link not found, or not utilised, in the brains of ordinary mortals.

Attempting to explain this phenomenon, some have pointed to the fact that sound and light both have wavelengths. Perhaps, therefore, their frequencies are proportionate in some way? The idea was mooted as early as the eighteenth century. But this was clutching at straws. Light is photonic radiation and can pass through the vacuum of space, while sound is carried through a medium, usually air, as a compression wave. This is why, as the cinema poster correctly put it, IN SPACE NO ONE CAN HEAR YOU SCREAM. Apart from this, the notion of a fixed physical correlation between sound and light, music and colour, is blown apart by the sheer inconsistency of synaesthetic individuals, who hear different colours for the same sounds.

One of the most fascinating examples of synaesthesia in music is the Russian pianist and composer Alexander Scriabin. His cherished dream was of an artform which would blend all five human senses in the ultimate mystical experience. His 1910 orchestral work *Prometheus, Poem of Fire* went some way towards that ideal. The orchestra includes a 'keyboard of light', whose keys produce coloured light rather than musical notes, the required spectrum being notated on its own stave in the full score, with pitches replaced by colours. During the performance the auditorium is bathed in whichever colour matches (according to Scriabin) the music at that point. As the music changes key, the colour changes with it.

The one performance I saw was a little underwhelming, it has to be said. Far from flooding the hall, the colours were projected on to a rectangular screen in a somewhat abrupt and desultory fashion, and the screen's brooding presence before the concert gave the impression that the conductor was intending to show us his holiday slides. There was meant to be some wafting fragrance too, but I detected nothing, and could only conclude that the waft didn't reach as far as the cheap seats...

Sound and light have always been a powerful double-act. God didn't write 'Let there be light'. He said it. In some creation stories, God sings the universe into existence. From the most tasteful National Trust *son et lumière*, to the brain-frying stroboscopes of the club down a road near you, the love affair between sound and light is as strong as ever. No one, though, has quite achieved the all-encompassing event imagined by Scriabin. The ultimate goal of his life was a 'supreme ecstatic mystery', planned to coincide with the final cataclysm marking the end of the world as we know it (one night only!). The work was never written. Just as well, perhaps.

II
Variations

Cornucopia

To compose is to paint on silence. Just as a painter applies colour within the frame of a blank canvas, so a composer applies sounds within a designated timeframe. But whereas a painting speaks for itself, without any further mediation, music needs instruments to bring it to life, with players to play them. Like a dramatic script without actors to play it out, a musical score unperformed is silent as the grave. And just like actors in a drama, musical instruments have their own characters, their own histories, roles and meanings.

Of all orchestral instruments, perhaps the one with the most potent symbolic baggage is the horn. For at least as long as the magic horn of Mahler's wandering youth (*Des Knaben Wunderhorn*) echoed through the German forests, other figures have been empowered by this primitive instrument – from Wagner's operatic character Siegfried to the fabled Little Boy Blue, and possibly even Little Jack Horner, who sensibly took time off from horn playing to eat his Christmas pie. It can be no accident, either, that the happily-named C S Forester gave his seafaring adventurer the name of Horatio Hornblower.

When we meet Siegfried in the third episode of Wagner's mighty four-night opera, *Der Ring des Nibelungen*, it is clear that the horn stands here for virility and heroism.

Siegfried's famed horn call proclaims his character, and Wagner knew he must get it right. It must have superheroic flair, yet be technically feasible. The most experienced composer may still consult a player of the instrument before committing his thoughts to paper, and this Wagner did. Siegfried's horn call was given a final polish by none other than Franz Strauss, principal horn in the Munich Court opera orchestra for forty-two years, a composer in his own right and the father of Richard Strauss. He was also a prominent opponent of Wagner, who regarded him as quite unbearable.

The French horn was named such in England, but there is little justification for this since the instrument, as we know it, was developed largely in Germany. Its pedigree stretches back to the times when animal horns were sounded in war, in the hunt or on ceremonial occasions. Replicas were made from other materials so that the fundamental note could be accurately determined. Cows or oxen, through no fault of their own, are not always perfectly in tune.

Throughout the era of Bach, Mozart and Beethoven, orchestral horns, usually a pair, were little more than coils of brass tubing, with no holes, and certainly no valves or pistons. For a piece written in the key of D, the horns could supply a low D, the fundamental, plus a limited range of overtones above this. The more skilled the player, the higher the overtones he could reach. Miraculous dexterity was achieved – as in Mozart horn concertos – but could not be relied upon. Most eighteenth-century parts for the orchestral horn are tedious in the extreme, merely adding weight and brassiness to loud passages.

So far, so good, but not all pieces are in D, though many were at that time. The next item in the programme might be in a higher key – F, say. In drastic circumstances, the new fundamental note, plus its harmonic series, might have been obtained by sawing off a portion of the tube. But this would be a somewhat hit-and-miss process, not to say disruptive in the middle of a concert. And anyway, what if a lower key was needed? The ingenious solution was to brace the tube in such a way that a separate metal loop, a crook, could be inserted as a short, extra segment of the tube, producing the requisite overall length.

An eighteenth-century horn player – or trumpet player, for that matter – would carry around with him a set of crooks designed to produce the keys most commonly used in the orchestral music of the time. When, in the 1830s, automatic valves were developed, orchestral players were slow to adopt them. Composers, too, continued to indicate crook changes up to the end of the nineteenth century, though some, like Berlioz, had experimented with the idea of using four or more horns, with a multiplicity of crooks, to achieve a wider range of notes within the same piece.

The conservative Brahms was one who still preferred the slightly raucous, outdoor sound of the natural horn, even with the inconvenience of crook changes. And indeed, modern, 'authentic' recordings have shown vividly how exciting that sound can be. In the finale of Brahms's first symphony, the principal horn has a prominent solo evoking the sound of the alphorn, a reminiscence of his holidays in the Swiss mountains. The real alphorn, one of many venerable ancestors of the modern horn, is an outdoor instrument whose sound can carry for miles. Its cumbersomely long, uncoiled tube is best handled by resting it on the slope of a convenient mountainside, within camera-reach of Japanese tourists.

If Brahms's suggested alphorn conjures up the splendour of the mountains with nobility and restraint, Richard Strauss meets a similar scenic challenge with characteristic musical gigantism. Perhaps it comes of having a professional horn player for a father – that grumpy old enemy of Wagner. The *Alpensinfonie* depicts a day in the mountains, around Strauss's villa in the Bavarian Alps, complete with cataract, cowbells, glacier, the view from the summit, mists, rain, a thunderstorm, sunset, and nightfall. To his already inflated orchestra, Strauss adds mechanical devices to evoke the sound of wind and thunder, organ, and no fewer than twenty – yes, twenty! – horns, creating an orchestral decibel level which in a factory would officially qualify as industrial sound-pollution.

At the opposite end of the spectrum from the heroic Siegfried, we find the horns of Strauss's orchestra glorifying the dissolute behaviour of Don Juan. This celebrated libertine had long held a fascination for composers, but not until Strauss had a purely orchestral sound been so graphic. Listen to the Don's theme in Strauss's youthful tone-poem of 1888, *Don Juan*. The first two notes say it all – a rising octave (G-G), blared out by the whole horn section in unison. Was there ever a theme so swaggeringly libidinous?

Strauss goes further in the prelude to his 1911 opera, *Der Rosenkavalier*. When the curtain rises on Act I, the Marschallin, the young wife of a mercifully absent field marshal, is in bed with the seventeen-year-old youth, Octavian. The fact that Octavian is also played by a woman cunningly introduces an extra frisson into the staid world of the German opera house, and one can imagine the ladies tutting with disapproval while the men slyly raised their opera glasses. It is morning and, as the lovers croon their post-coital adoration, we understand retrospectively what all that pre-curtain orchestral romping was about. The short but vigorous prelude is full of the plunging and swooning phrases that are a hallmark of Strauss, and at the climax the whole horn section emits a series of ecstatic whoops, perhaps the nearest that the chaste art of music can approach to pornography.

We have swung from the heroic to the priapic (horny, if you prefer) but the horn still has other facets to its character. For all its sophisticated gadgetry, its finely-machined, twelve-foot tube, and its smoothly-operating rotary valves, composers have sometimes been drawn back to the rawness of its ancient forbears. In his oratorio *The Apostles*, Elgar evokes the sound of the *shofar*, a ram's horn used in the early Jewish synagogue, but not easily found in Edwardian England. Britten, in his *Spring Symphony*, stipulates the use of a cow horn to lend bucolic flavour to his joyous finale, which features the famous mediaeval canon *Summer is icumen in*.

In another recreation of an older, simpler sound, Britten's *Serenade for Tenor, Horn and Strings* begins with an unaccompanied horn passage to be played using only the natural harmonics of the instrument, despite some of them being out of tune. Later in the work the horn does service as a bugle for Tennyson's lines 'Blow, bugle, blow'. The same thing happens in Britten's *War Requiem*, to illustrate the words of the World War I poet Wilfred Owen:

> Bugles sang, sadd'ning the evening air;
> And bugles answered, sorrowful to hear.

Only in Britten's *Noyes Fludde*, a community stage-work involving hordes of children, is there a part for real bugles, played, he hoped, by the local Boys' Brigade as a cheerfully anachronistic accompaniment to the animals entering the ark.

At the very end of his elegiac *Serenade for Tenor, Horn and Strings*, the opening horn solo returns as an epilogue, complete with out-of-tune natural harmonics. This time the passage is to be played offstage – a typically brilliant *coup de théâtre*. With the player invisible, the sound takes on a disembodied, elemental quality, seeming to disappear into the very fabric of the building. It's one of the great musical endings.

The pitch and tone of the horn are normally refined by the insertion of the player's right hand into the bell of the instrument, hence the name hand horn. There the hand stays throughout the performance, supporting the weight of the horn and subtly regulating the flow of air. The hand may be pressed right into the bell, creating a muted effect, magical when soft, acidly pungent when loud. The general direction of a horn player's sound is backwards, as I discovered as a child, sitting in the Royal Albert Hall choir seats behind the orchestra, when I was exposed to Beethoven's rollicking, rackety *Seventh Symphony*.

Occasionally, composers have instructed the player to hold the instrument aloft, disengaging the right hand entirely, so that the bell points more directly to the audience. This is invariably used for very loud passages needing a brash, blaring tone. 'Bell in the air', the score tells us. '*Campana in aria*' is the mellifluous Italian phrase. The French suggestively murmur '*Pavillon en l'air*', while Austro-German composers, adopting a more bossy tone, bark '*Schalltrichter auf!*' – 'Bell up!'

Such gimmicks are a symptom of the expansion of the twentieth-century orchestra. With an army of players generating a deluge of sound, horn players may sometimes be asked to let rip in this startling way, deliberately ruining the tone-quality and intonation they have tried for so many years to cultivate. Stand up, the guilty men! And any female composers who will admit to this kind of rowdy behaviour! The evidence is there for all to hear: Gustav Mahler in various symphonies; Igor Stravinsky, *Ritual Action of the Ancestors* (Part 2 of *The Rite of Spring*); Aaron Copland in his *Symphony No. 3*. There are others too (you know who you are). Well, let's be magnanimous. Let's concede that a temporary loss of tone-quality and control are a small price to pay for the sheer visceral excitement, so long as you're not standing too close.

When the player's right hand, normally used to refine the intonation, is pressed into the bell to mute the sound, the sounding-length of the tube is shortened, and the pitch of the note rises a semitone. If, however, a cupped hand is held just in front of the bell, the air-column in the tube is effectively extended. The note will, with luck, slide down a semitone, while the tone grows muffled. While writing his *Serenade for Tenor, Horn and Strings* for Dennis Brain, the greatest horn virtuoso of his day, Britten must have been avid to learn all he could about horn techniques from the master. This effect is his trump card, and must have sent shivers down the spines of the first audience to hear it. With Britten's skill, Blake's brief poem about a sick rose, over whose sexual symbolism literary critics have long panted, is turned into a haunting elegy:

> O rose, thou art sick!
> The invisible worm
> That flies in the night,
> In the howling storm,
> Has found out thy bed
> Of crimson joy,
> And his dark secret love
> Does thy life destroy.

Chilling stuff! Add the music and it's enough to make the hardiest gardener blanch. In the dying moments, the solo horn oscillates between a G# (G-sharp), a normal, open tone, and the G a semitone lower, a stifled, half-muted tone. The slow slide of pitch, back and forth between these two notes, can induce real queasiness as the listener's thoughts waver between 'How on earth do they do that?' and 'My God, that rose is sick! Let us spray before it's too late.'

The modern, professional horn player is capable of many novel effects, and the modern composer has been quick to exploit them. Even chords are possible. If you play one note and hum another at the same time – easier said than done – a third, higher note should appear as the summation frequency, creating a three-part chord. The English-born composer Richard Rodney Bennett used this technique to dramatic effect in his *Actaeon* for horn and orchestra. An impressive party trick, but of limited application.

Night and darkness are the natural haunt of the horn, and nowhere is it more at home than in *A Midsummer Night's Dream*. Deep in Shakespeare's enchanted wood, it reconnects with its ancient roots of hunting and magic. Mendelssohn, in his incidental music for the play, created one of the most famous of all horn solos, *The Nocturne*, during which Puck anoints the sleeping lovers' eyes with the potent juice of a flower. Britten's operatic score for this play takes us to the same enchanted wood. As the lovers awake, there is a distant offstage sound of hunting horns, which taps into a long musical tradition stretching back to Berlioz's *The Trojans*, and beyond.

And yet, setting aside all this mystery and magic, perhaps the most refreshing feature of the horn is the way it can cast dignity to the winds and misbehave, revelling in its bovine pedigree. In comic opera, for example, it is inevitable that when an attractive young wife is married to a crusty older man, she will betray him. And when she does, or threatens to, the cuckolded husband will be forcibly reminded of his plight by a pair of horns in the orchestra. Just as Shakespeare's cuckoo 'mocks married men', so composers like Mozart (for instance, in Figaro's aria in Act IV of *The Marriage of Figaro*) are always ready with the 'horns of cuckoldry'. 'Tarra-TAH, tarra-TAH, tarra-TAH', we hear, as the timeless taunt of a pair of fingers held to the brow (a relative of the V-sign) erupts brazenly in the genteel eighteenth-century orchestra. How the ladies must have tittered behind their fans! Like a swear word in polite company, a brace of braying natural horns is hard to ignore.

Bracing Brass

In all honesty, what is a trumpet but a higher-pitched horn? In baroque and classical music, both instruments used crooks. The only thing that really distinguished them was the length and bore of the tube, the flare of the bell, and the type of mouthpiece. For a player, though, moving from one to another was not as easy as stepping into a new pair of shoes. The manner of blowing, or embouchure, was as critical as it is today and the facial muscles would need time to adapt. In essence, though, the player was simply blowing into a metal tube (sorry, I withdraw that 'simply'), so as to isolate the required notes in the harmonic series.

Like other technologies, the development of musical instruments went forward in fits and starts. Some ideas bore fruit, but many didn't. Haydn's popular *Trumpet Concerto* of 1796 was written for a prototype trumpet, with keys covering the finger holes, but the design fell by the wayside, and players returned to their crooked ways until the automated piston-valve finally caught on.

Trombones are a special case. The notion of a tube made instantly adjustable by a slide may date back as far as the fourteenth-century. The instrument was much favoured in Tudor England, where it was known as a sackbut or, more delightfully, a saggbutt, or even a shagbolt. A whole family of alto, tenor and bass trombones, and even soprano ones, survived till the early years of the nineteenth century, after which only the tenor and bass remained as standard, while the smaller, higher versions continued on their well-oiled slide to obscurity.

The brilliantly simple concept of using a slide instead of a crook should have been the answer to all problems, but in practice it wasn't. In 1694, when Queen Mary, the popular wife of William III of Orange, succumbed to smallpox at the age of thirty-two, the music for her elaborate funeral in Westminster Abbey included an anthem 'accompanied with flat Mournful

Trumpets'. This is not a reference to the poor intonation of the players. Flat or flatt trumpets, characterised by a slide moving backwards over the player's shoulder, had been introduced to London in 1691 by the Moravian composer, Gottfried Finger.

So what was Finger's big idea? Well, you may recall that the first few notes of the harmonic series make a major chord, notes which add brassy highlights to many a triumphant cadence. Try listening to Bach's *Orchestral Suite No. 3 in D* – the bits that are not the famous cigar-smoking air! Think of the *Hallelujah* chorus from Handel's *Messiah*. A good time is had by all, in D major again. But funerals demand solemnity. And solemnity means minor keys. However, the notes of a minor scale are not available on instruments which depend solely on the harmonic series. Unless those instruments have a slide.

Gottfried Finger's slide-equipped flatt trumpets, used for Purcell's minor-key funeral anthem, were one answer. It's hard to see how they differed much from their forbears, the sackbuts, except for the backwards direction of the slide, which may have proved hazardous in a crowded Westminster Abbey. At any rate the idea fell flat. Queen Mary's funeral seems to have been the pinnacle of their brief career, and Finger's print on musical history is a faint one.

By the seventeenth-century, the trombone, or sackbut, had long been associated with death and mourning. In Monteverdi's 1607 opera, *L'Orfeo*, trombones accompany Orpheus on his descent into the underworld. They appear too at the climax of Mozart's *Don Giovanni* (1787), when the grim, avenging statue of the Commendatore lurches into the Don's supper party, hell gapes and *il dissoluto* is well and truly *punito*.

In the *Requiem* too, Mozart's final, uncompleted work, trombones paint the shadows in the orchestral picture, and, curiously, it is even a trombone that calls the dead to judgement. To confuse things further, the Latin word for a trumpet is tuba. '*Tuba mirum spargens sonum... coget omnes ante thronum*' says the Latin text: 'The trumpet spreading far its wondrous sound summons all before the throne'. The tuba as we know it didn't exist when those words were written, though the thought of a plump angel Gabriel waking the dead with a blast on the tuba is appealing!

For Mozart, the sombre trombone was a fair substitute for the last trump. At least it could play the notes he wanted. Beginning with a broken chord of B♭ which, taken out of context, can sound less like the angel Gabriel than Uncle Fred warming up for the local band practice, it launches into a brief, but rather precarious, duet with the bass soloist, using many notes that were unplayable on the trumpet of Mozart's time.

A lot can happen in a hundred years, though. Verdi in his 1874 *Requiem* makes a more Italianate meal of the same eschatological moment. A mighty cohort of offstage trumpets – actual trumpets this time, presumably equipped like Gabriel's with the latest in valve technology – begins its summons in the far distance, then grows in power till an ear-shattering fanfare, interestingly in a minor key, seems to thrill through the entire universe. One of the most hair-raising moments in all music!

Everyone loves the thrill of a high note, and solo trumpet parts are often obliging in that respect. The note itself may not be more intrinsically beautiful than a lower one, but the element of danger sets pulses racing. Added to which, the trumpet sound has always dazzled listeners. It is the gold leaf on the orchestral picture. No composer has extracted more from the trumpet than Handel, especially when one considers the crippling technical limitations of the period. Many people are familiar with the bass aria 'The Trumpet Shall Sound' from *Messiah*, but try for a change 'Let the Bright Seraphim' from the oratorio *Samson*, in which the trumpet engages the solo soprano in a glittering musical duel. The words are from Milton:

> Let the bright seraphim in burning row
> Their loud, uplifted angel trumpets blow.

Or, more stratospheric still, look out for the purely instrumental showpiece, Bach's *Brandenburg Concerto No. 2*. These works come from a golden age when clarino trumpeters, specialists in the ultra-high register, drew commensurately high salaries in the court ensembles of Europe. In the politically unstable time of Haydn and Mozart, when aristocratic households made budget cuts, these specialist skills died. The clarino party was over and nobody got that high anymore. Hence the somewhat earthbound trumpet-parts of the classical orchestra.

The lustre of the trumpet reflects terrestrial armies as well as the angelic host. 'If the trumpet give an uncertain sound, who shall prepare himself to the battle?' asked Saint Paul, who understood the bracing power of brass when loins must be girded for the fight. Handel too had an equal appetite for the celestial and the military. In his *Ode on Saint Cecilia's Day*, the trumpet performs its usual double act with drums, whose double-beat rhythm is prefigured in Dryden's rattling piece of onomatopoeia. Can you read lines five and six aloud without hearing a deafening military tattoo?

> The trumpet's loud clangour
> Excites us to arms,
> With shrill notes of anger,
> And mortal alarms.
> The double double double beat
> Of the thundering drum
> Cries Hark! the foes come;
> Charge, charge, 'tis too late to retreat!

Musicians cherish the old story of the hapless offstage trumpeter in one performance of Beethoven's 'rescue opera', *Fidelio*. In the final act, catastrophe is averted in the nick of time by the government minister, whose cortege is heard in the distance. The offstage trumpet call, heralding his arrival, is one of the most dramatic interventions in all opera, a forerunner of the US-cavalry moment in the final reel of a John Wayne movie. The chosen trumpeter, having been placed in some remote part of the theatre, was raising the instrument to his lips when a heavy hand was clapped on his shoulder. 'You can't play that blooming trumpet 'ere, sir,' hissed a theatre official, bustling him away. 'Don't you know there's an opera going on?' '*Se non e vero e ben trovato*,' as the Italians say: 'If it's not true, it should be.'

Composers don't usually do multiple trumpets in the way they do multiple horns, but one exception is the 1926 *Sinfonietta* by Janacek, which calls for twelve trumpets, including two of that rare breed, the bass trumpet. This case of overkill was brought on by a forgivable surge of national pride in the new Czech homeland. The work as a whole was dedicated to the Czech army, though the opening fanfare had its origins in music Janacek wrote for an outdoor gymnastics festival. Is it my imagination, or does it still exude a faint odour of changing rooms and massed keep-fit classes?

The trumpet's origins are lost in history. In a gesture towards remote antiquity, Verdi calls for straight (uncoiled) trumpets in the triumphal scene that closes Act II of *Aida* (1870). We are in the time of the Pharaohs. As the Egyptian hero Radames returns from routing the Ethiopians, his choral and orchestral reception is burnished by two groups of onstage trumpets, one group pitched a third higher than the other. The tune of the grand march is played through in A♭, by the first group, then the pitch is hoisted for the repeat of the tune in B, by the second group. Since both keys share certain notes, all the trumpets may join together as well. Good planning on Verdi's part, for the effect is electrifying.

Strange to relate, when someone finally got round to playing the two bronze trumpets unearthed in 1922 by Howard Carter, from the tomb of the boy-pharaoh, Tutankhamen, they were found to be pitched in two different keys. And as they listened to those thin, unearthly notes breaking a silence of three and a half thousand years, they realised that the keys were A♭ and B. Spooky, eh?

In his symphonic poem, *The Pines of Rome* (1924), Verdi's later compatriot Ottorino Respighi calls for six *buccinae*, or ancient Roman natural trumpets – a real headache for the orchestral manager who must also track down a recording of a nightingale, to be played during the nocturnal third movement. Respighi is a wonderful orchestrator and his wishes must be respected, but from the point of view of recreating the sound of a marching Roman army, fitting six *buccinae* into a twentieth-century orchestra is about as authentic as fitting wagon wheels on to a top-of-the-range BMW. Quibbles apart, the lumbering approach of Respighi's ancient Roman army is overwhelming. Did you know, by the way, that the word 'orchestra' is an anagram of 'carthorse'?

The trumpet and the horn both have a certain flashiness.

Trombones can be showy at times too, as the prelude to the third act of Wagner's *Lohengrin* attests. How unfair, though, that the tuba is so often dismissed as the comedian of the orchestra. For those of a certain age, this comic image was indelibly etched in our minds by the musical tale *Tubby the Tuba*, endlessly played on children's request programmes in the 1950s. Doing stalwart service at the bottom end of the brass, it varies widely in size and pitch. But its Billy Bunter bulk belies its expressive tone and delicacy, and like many rotund individuals, it is surprisingly light on its feet. It's even been given the odd solo. One of the best known is the *Bydlo* (ox-cart) movement in Mussorgsky's *Pictures at an Exhibition*, as orchestrated by Ravel. The high pitch of this solo, however, means that many players feel safer using the smaller tuba, the sort known in brass bands as the euphonium.

Orchestral roads of the nineteenth century are paved with brass, and most of those roads lead to Richard Wagner. As well as writing words and music for his gargantuan operas, directing and conducting them, writing books about them, and designing a state-of-the-art theatre in which to house them, the tireless Wagner took a few minutes off to come up with a new type of tuba. More of a compromise between a tuba and a horn, it evolved from ideas Wagner had when looking round the work-shops of Adolphe Sax, inventor of the saxophone. A slight nudge to the turning wheel of history and Wagner might have been a forerunner of Charlie Parker, in addition to his other achieve-ments. But it was not to be. The so-called Wagner tuba, weightier in every sense than the giddy and groovy saxophone, became a fitting memorial to a man whose reputation remains the weighti-est in music history.

Four of these tubas, doubled by four of the regular horn play-ers, lend extra weight to the brass in his *Ring Cycle*. They crop up too in the seventh and ninth symphonies of Bruckner, a devout worshipper at the Wagner shrine. Strauss used them in his opera *Elektra*. Even Stravinsky, who complained that he desperately needed a cigarette during the long acts of a Wagner opera, acceded to a suggestion by the conductor Ernest Ansermet that two of the horn players in the *Rite of Spring* should double on Wagner tubas, to achieve more carrying power. Sharp-eyed concert-goers may spot them switching instruments in mid-flow. But the Wagner tuba is a rare beast and shows little sign of eclipsing the saxophone – unless, perhaps, there's a small club somewhere in Bavaria?

A fair number of instruments lead a double life in both wind band, or jazz band, and orchestra. The saxophone is one. Adolphe Sax, one answer to the perennial challenge to name a famous Belgian, constructed his eponymous instrument as something of a hybrid, with a metal body and a single-reed mouthpiece, as on the clarinet. As with other moonlighting musicians, players of the saxophone tend to match their tone-quality to their surroundings. In an orchestra they blend with the woodwind rather self-consciously, like a fully made-up nightclub singer doing her shopping in Tesco. In Vaughan Williams' ballet, *Job*, the saxo-phone plays the part of Job's comforters, oozing self-righteousness. Let them loose in a jazz band and what happens? They relax into a sleazy vibrato, and start to form raunchy relationships with the brass.

The cornet is another rare migrant occasionally glimpsed in the orchestra. There is little it can do that cannot be done by its cousin, the trumpet, but very rapid tonguing, causing repetition of a single note, is one of its party turns. A star of the wind band, it will play banal variations, with plenty of machine-gun triple-tonguing, on an even more banal theme till the cows come home. Its role in the orchestra is limited to more folksy moments in works such as Tchaikovsky's *Capriccio Italien*, or Stravinsky's *Petrushka* (*The Ballerina's Dance*). Its agile and silvery tone fit it for passages with a certain circus-like glitz.

The cornet (accent on the first syllable) is not to be confused with the cornett (accent on the second syllable, please). The cornett, or *cornetto* in Italian, belongs to a family of Renaissance wind instruments, revived by early music enthusiasts for the authentic performance of music by Gabrieli, Monteverdi and the like. The body was wooden, usually curved, sometimes covered in leather, and had holes not unlike the recorder. The cupped mouthpiece was brass. It is heard in the introductory flourish to Monteverdi's opera *L'Orfeo* and in the opening of the same composer's *Vespers* (1610), which has identical music. Beware of mentioning the cornet – a Johnny-come-lately, whose first orchestral appearance was probably in Rossini's 1829 opera, *William Tell* – in the company of early music specialists, who think, speak and probably dream only of cornetts. All kinds of unpleasantness could ensue. At least now a new generation of players has mastered (just about) the vagaries of the strangely plangent cornett. No longer can it be called an ill wind that nobody blows any good!

When all is said and done, the brass family is a set of variations on a metal tube. Its versatility is breathtaking – literally. So, despite the vast range of solemn and uplifting music it has inspired, we should not be too shocked to find the odd family member playing mundane, even rather ignominious, character parts when pressed, or perhaps blown, by circumstances.

In the last act of Britten's opera *Peter Grimes* there is a crucial non-singing role that helps drive the action to its tragic conclusion. Not the doomed fisherman himself, not the widow Ellen Orford, not the villagers baying for blood, not even the brooding presence of the sea. No, the really indispensable component in that final scene, where Grimes staggers alone on to the stage, his mind disintegrating, is a foghorn. And the part of this unseen foghorn, booming from far out to sea, is played by a tuba. Britten gives it an E ♭ to play, but, with his usual meticulousness, marks a slight droop at the end of the note. A Doppler-effect concession to naturalism that lifts this dumpy instrument out of the orchestra pit, and raises it to the status of a key player in the drama.

In a jollier way, that more demotic English composer, Malcolm Arnold, does a similar thing in his rousing march, *The Padstow Lifeboat*. There in the thick of the musical texture, gloriously and deliberately out of tune with everything else, is the sound of the fog signal at Trevose Head, not far from where Arnold lived, near Padstow in Cornwall. The original device, erected by Trinity House and in use until 1964, was a gigantic mechanised hooter, thirty-six feet long, giving warning blasts to shipping over a wide area.

And on the subject of sirens and hooters – raising the pitch, but lowering the tone – what of those more modest, hand-powered klaxons that feature in the pantomime drummer's repertoire of funny noises? In his orchestral score *An American in*

Paris, George Gershwin calls for a quartet of variously-tuned klaxons to honk rudely, but in precisely notated rhythms, across the sound of the orchestra, denoting the busy traffic of the French capital in the 1920s.

At last, we have stumbled on a genuine example of the French horn, as played at rush hour by Parisian taxi-drivers.

Bells and Whistles

One version of the Pythagoras story has the great philosopher passing a smithy and hearing the sound of various anvils being struck. Listening carefully to the notes produced by the struck metal, he himself was struck – by an idea! Further research revealed that a slab of metal half the size of another slab would create a note one octave higher when struck. The slabs were in harmonic sympathy. Another slab, a third the size of the first, made a note an octave and a fifth higher. And a quarter-size slab sounded two octaves above the original. These slabs of metal, not unlike keys on a modern glockenspiel, worked in the same way as a vibrating monochord, stacking up notes in a tidy mathematical pattern – a half, a third, a quarter, a fifth and so on – which matched the harmonic series of any given note.

In its simplest terms, a bell is a piece of struck metal, and early man must have noticed the ringing sound when he dropped his wife's best bronze pot on the ground. It doesn't take a great imaginative leap to suspend a graduated line of metal objects so that they vibrate freely when struck. In the Middle Ages, plain-chant melodies were sometimes sung with a set of dinky bells doubling the vocal line, a lovely thought which chimes well with the mediaeval love of colour in clothes, tapestries and frescoes.

From that time on, our lives have been regulated by bells. Even in our electronic age, real bells continue to bless marriages, and our final exit may be made to the same muffled peal as that of our forefathers. Church bells were even thought to affect the weather, banish plague, extinguish fires, and, as recently as World War II, stood by to warn of enemy invasion. Miniature bells have kept us in touch with our livestock, with errant cats, and with hunting falcons. The sanctus bell, which marks the transubstantiation of the Host at High Mass, might equally prompt Pavlov's dogs to dribble for their dinner. Time itself has been tamed by chiming clocks. Schools, ships, factories, and even pubs have all bowed to the decree of bells great and small.

Bells have a special place in English life. Other countries have forged heavier, deeper bells, but the English country church has long prided itself on the craft of change-ringing by rope and wheel. Traditional peals, rejoicing in such names as Bob Major and Grandsire Triples, are rung out by teams of enthusiasts over many hours, until every permutation, often running into the thousands, is completely exhausted – not to mention the ringers themselves! It's as English as morris dancing, and about as impenetrable to foreign tourists. The bass-line of Purcell's cheery anthem, *Rejoice in the Lord Alway*, usually known as the *Bell Anthem*, traces the falling patterns of English bell-ringing. And three centuries after it was written, the practice is still hale and hearty.

Inscriptions on the bells remind us of their timeless involvement with life and death. '*Mortuos plango! Vivos voco!*' proclaims the great bell of Winchester Cathedral. 'I mourn the dead! I call the living!' This provided the title for a 1980 work by Jonathan Harvey, in which a boy's treble voice is blended with the electronically sampled bell itself. In country churches, regulations were posted warning the ringers to behave themselves. One such notice, dated 1907, from St Keverne's Church in Cornwall, reads:

> Who swears or curses, or in choleric mood
> Quarrels or strikes altho' he draws no blood,
> Who wears his hat or spur, or o'erturns a bell
> Or by unskilful handling marrs a peal,
> Let him pay 6d for each single crime,
> 'Twill make him cautious 'gainst another time.

It certainly will. Bells have a certain dignity, and ringing them demands sobriety and concentration. Their pervasive influence is the subject of Edgar Allan Poe's poem, *The Bells*, set to music (in a Russian version) by Rachmaninov. In the first movement, the silver of sleigh-bells on a starry night symbolises birth. Next, marriage is celebrated with golden bells. Brazen bells sound an alarm, inspiring fear and grief, and finally a single iron bell tolls out a funeral knell. Just the thing to appeal to the melancholy

Rachmaninov, described as 'six foot two of Russian gloom' by Stravinsky, who was not exactly the life and soul of the party himself.

Considering the hard labour of their manufacture, their longevity, their gratifying resistance to scientific analysis, and the power they wield in human affairs, it's not surprising that church bells have been invested with human, even criminal tendencies. In the 1934 novel, *The Nine Tailors*, by English writer Dorothy L Sayers, the patrician detective-hero, Lord Peter Wimsey, puts himself in grave danger by climbing the tower and entering the ringing-chamber in mid-peal, demonstrating almost too effectively how church bells, joyous and musical at a safe distance, can at close quarters become instruments of death.

Bells can add a splash of colour to orchestral works. Their pitch too is a bit of a splash. A profusion of harmonics makes the initial 'strike note' hard to pin down, and as it fades, a lower 'hum note' becomes audible. The real pitch can be unclear unless the bell is used with other instruments. A full modern percussion section will have tubular bells, a graduated set of steel tubes suspended from a frame, which are struck with a mallet, but the problem for composers seeking a seriously deep bell-tone is that tubular bells sound very much like, well, tubular bells. That means something like a suburban door-chime. And not that low either. The longest one only sounds at about middle C. Surprisingly, even Big Ben, the hour bell of the famous Westminster chimes, only gets a bit lower, and that weighs in at something over thirteen tons! In his *London Symphony*, Vaughan Williams wisely opts for the distant effect using just harp and clarinet.

High-pitched bells are less of a problem, and many a musical sleigh-ride has included a part for shaken jingles of indeterminate pitch. Mahler's *Fourth Symphony* begins with this sound, though, with Mahler being Mahler, they are likely to presage DEATH rather than a nice outing in the snow. The triangle is a familiar example of a high-pitched metal instrument with no fixed note. High bell-sounds of a specific pitch are usually the preserve of the glockenspiel, a grown-up version of the school chime-bars, set out like a piano keyboard and played with mallets.

Its relative, the xylophone, which has wooden keys, gives out the brittle sound of the dancing fossils in *Carnival of the Animals*, by Saint-Saens, while its more sophisticated cousin, the vibraphone, has a resonating tube attached to each note, inside which a spinning fan, driven by a motor, alternately opens and closes the tube. This imparts that bilious wobble, for ever associated with rather miserable 1960s-type jazz, the sort used in monochrome films about bad housing and unmarried mothers.

Far more other-worldly is the sound of the miniature percussion instrument, known in English as antique cymbals. Their French name, *crotales*, with its overtones of a rather unpleasant rash, should not put us off. Sparingly and magically featured towards the end of Debussy's *Prelude à l'après-midi d'un faune*, they are really pairs of fairy-sized cymbals struck delicately together. Each pair creates a fairy-sized note, very high and faint, but definite in pitch and of surpassing sweetness.

Composers have often preferred 'orchestrated' bell-sounds to the real thing, making up their own recipe from a skilful blend of other instruments. My own favourite is Vaughan Williams's tolling bell in his 1909 song-cycle, *On Wenlock Edge*, for solo tenor, piano and string quartet. The piano plays an octave-G around middle C, but the ictus, or strike, of the note, which would betray it as a piano sound, is covered by a plucked violin G. So simple, but if well played it is as startling an evocation of a distant bell as you could wish for. As part of the musical landscape for Housman's tragic verse (from *A Shropshire Lad*) it can be heartbreaking.

> They tolled the one bell only,
> Groom there was none to see,
> The mourners followed after,
> And so to church went she,
> And would not wait for me.

Large orchestral bells are where the trouble starts. The pitches notated by Berlioz in the demonic finale of his *Symphonie Fantastique* would require bells large enough to take up most of the stage, and probably demolish it into the bargain. Tubular bells have neither the depth nor the sense of menace for these notes, and a compromise of a pair of large *bell-shaped* bells is the best that can be managed. Nowadays, CD recordings may have a deep bell sound edited in later, but the effect can so easily suggest a Hammer horror film spoof: 'You RANG, sir?'

The coronation scene in Mussorgsky's opera, *Boris Godunov*, is justly famous for its clamorous Russian bells, made the more imposing by the visual impact of the scene, and by the overall tumult of choir and orchestra. *Parsifal* is even more of a challenge. As Wagner's Knights of the Grail process to their celebration of Holy Communion, bells in the orchestra sound a solemn motif of four notes, notated at an impractically deep pitch. Various solutions have been tried in live performances, not least at the annual Bayreuth Wagner festival where one solution to the *Parsifal* bell problem was an instrument said to resemble something between an iron bedstead and a billiard table, only noisier. Tuned gongs, like those in Puccini's opera, *Madam Butterfly*, only lower in pitch, are a more practical solution.

The piano has been given more bell effects than any other instrument, especially by French impressionist composers. Truly wonderful things have been achieved in this way, none more so than Ravel's *Vallée des cloches*, the last movement of his *Miroirs* (1905). The soft, hazy blend of many different peals, coming from all points of the compass across a dreaming summer landscape, is a masterly piece of writing for the piano, and a challenge to any player. Percy Grainger's orchestral arrangement of the piece, with its array of real bells, seems pedestrian by comparison. Subtle suggestion wins every time over slavish imitation. The Italian Respighi, no blushing wallflower when it comes to laying on orchestral colour, had more justification in his *Feste Romane*, or *Roman Festivals*. He goes to town in every sense: tubular bells, carillon, harps, celesta, and piano duet, not to mention cymbals, jingles and rattle, all making up the chaotic sounds of the Eternal City at festival time.

In Mozart's *Magic Flute*, the absurd figure of Papageno, already encumbered with a birdcage, has also to cope with bells and pipes. A five-note set of pipes announces him as a rustic simpleton. The bells, however, given to him by the mysterious Three Ladies, have magical powers and can set people dancing uncontrollably, a handy attribute in moments of danger. Emanuel Schikaneder, the comic actor who also wrote the libretto and created the part of Papageno for himself, was as big a draw as the music. But even he could be duped. While the show played to packed houses, Mozart would creep into the orchestra and indulge his love of silly tricks, improvising flourishes on the keyed glockenspiel to confuse poor Schikaneder as he tried to match his stage movements to the bells.

Papageno is a naive, instinctive creature, not used to human society. His pipes recall the pan pipes played by the mythological Greek nature-god, Pan, a lusty creature, half-man and half-goat. Anyone who ventured into his Arcadian realm might well be gripped by that special fear called panic. Pan loved the nymph Syrinx, but she resisted his advances. Taking pity on her, the river-nymphs turned her into a reed, and Pan's desires were thwarted. All he could do was to pluck her and play on her, which is why panpipes are known by the name syrinx.

The flute, a descendant of the pan pipes, often paints a picture of a halcyon time of nymphs, and fauns, and shepherds in a sun-drenched Mediterranean landscape. Of his ballet score, *Daphnis and Chloë*, Ravel wrote that he was less concerned with archaism than with faithfully reproducing the Greece of his dreams. Listen to the languorous flute solo that follows the sunrise music, and dream on happily. A similarly Arcadian scene occurs in Gluck's opera, *Orfeo ed Euridice*, when Orpheus arrives in the Elysian Fields of the afterlife seeking his beloved Euridice. Here in the *Dance of the Blessed Spirits*, we meet the ethereal flute solo so admired by Berlioz. The legend of Orpheus, the divine singer of myth, has always preoccupied opera composers, but he is also a string-player, as we shall see.

At the time of Gluck's opera, the flute was still quite primitive, blown in a crossways manner, but with a chunky wooden body and holes much like a recorder. Definitions were so loose then that it is often unclear which a composer intends to be played, the end-blown recorder or the crossways flute. Bach's *Fourth Brandenburg Concerto* is a case in point. More helpful scores specify *flute à bec*, the recorder, or *flauto traverso*, the crossways flute. The latter edged ahead of its rival, and little by little its key-work proliferated. Wood gave way to metal, and the homely body slimmed down to a svelte gleaming wand. A modern flute may be plated with silver, or even gold, further enhancing its aristocratic status. Platinum flutes have been made too, and it was for one of these that the French-American composer Edgar Varèse wrote his *Density 21.5* (1936), the title referring enigmatically to the density of platinum.

The sound of the flute is wild and free. Despite all those pious Lutheran cantatas of Bach, in which a flute wreathes dutiful baroque decorations around a soulful Christian voice, it has never quite shed its pagan associations. Think of the secular Handel arias, where a flute (or perhaps a recorder) gives a protracted impression of birdsong in some sylvan grove. Think of such scantily-clad flute trios as the *Egyptian Dance* in Verdi's *Aida*, and the *Danse des Mirlitons* in Tchaikovsky's *Nutcracker* ballet. Or perhaps Messiaen's *Le Merle Noir*, an ornithological tour de force for solo flute and piano. Ravishing as all these are, it is Debussy's three-minute essay, *Syrinx*, for a single unaccompanied flute that shows us the true pagan nature of the instrument – solitary, sensuous, sweet, passionate – a wandering voice redolent of all ancient, lonely places.

The flute, or pipe, is still a mainstay of folk music. James Galway began his musical career by playing the tin-whistle in Irish bands, before making the leap to the world of classical music and playing under Herbert von Karajan as principal flute in the Berlin Philharmonic. In Shakespeare's time a popular entertainment was the pipe and tabor, the three-hole pipe and the small drum being played simultaneously by one performer, with a bit of dancing thrown in for good measure. Nowadays, as a member of the Musicians' Union, this ambidextrous player might demand a double fee.

And let's not forget the bagpipes, another instrument of the open air – the more open the better! This ancient device – by no means confined to Scotland, but found all over the world in various shapes and sizes – requires a special technique, whereby air is kept under pressure in a bag and constantly replenished by the player's puff. Its two pipes, a chanter for the tune and a drone to provide a single sustained note, are a distant echo of the Greek *aulos*, a double-flute seen on ancient Greek vases, piping to the spirit ditties of no tone, as Keats observed. And where would Browning's Pied Piper have been without his pipe?

> Into the street the Piper stept,
> Smiling first a little smile,
> As if he knew what magic slept
> In his quiet pipe the while;
> Then like a musical adept,
> To blow the pipe his lips he wrinkled,
> And green and blue his sharp eyes twinkled,
> Like a candle-flame where salt is sprinkled.

This strange figure, with his long coat, half of yellow and half of red, had no recourse to pesticides when ridding the town of Hamelin of its rats. The pipe did the trick. Music mesmerises. Pipes mean power. The rats followed the piebald stranger to their deaths. But when he was denied his rightful fee, the piper piped away the town's children as well. Let that be a lesson to all mayors and corporations. The workman – and that includes musicians – is worthy of his hire.

Every Saturday afternoon whistles come out to play. The common pea variety is a vital part of the soccer referee's equipment. And what games mistress, what railway guard, what French gendarme would be complete without the statutory whistle? In the glory days of the British Navy, the boatswain summoned the crew to their tasks with his boatswain's whistle, and the same simple instrument still pipes senior ranks aboard today.

One doesn't even need an instrument to whistle. The Irish composer and conductor, Hamilton Harty, would always whistle in rehearsals to show how he wanted a phrase played – very much preferable to the usual groan of the emoting conductor. And though it seems odd to us now, there was a time when popular vocalists, like Bing Crosby, who made a career of groaning, also whistled professionally.

The amateur form, the wolf whistle, perfected by building workers the world over, though its connection with wolves is puzzling, remains largely a male thing, perhaps because the necessary lip-pursing is open to misinterpretation if performed by women. You may recall the helpful advice given to Humphrey Bogart by Lauren Bacall: 'If you want anything, just whistle. You know how to whistle, don't you?' – here Miss Bacall's eyelids took on a sexy droop – 'Just put your lips together and blow.'

To breathe into an instrument is to animate it, to bring it to life with the *anima* – the breath, soul or spirit. Breath is life, and it is not for nothing that God breathed into Adam's nostrils. But blowing into a pipe can unleash destructive forces too. In M R James's ghost story, *Oh Whistle, and I'll Come to You, My lad!*, an ancient pipe is dug up bearing that inscription. Needless to say, someone is tempted to try a note or two, but what it is that comes (my lad!) I shall leave you the delicious thrill of finding out by yourself.

Many woodwind instruments – like the oboe, the clarinet, the saxophone, the bassoon – need the help of vibrating reeds to animate them. The flute uses edge-tone. The breath, directed across a hole, is split in two by the opposite edge, and sets the air-column in motion, just like blowing across the top of a bottle. The whistle and the recorder are blown directly through a lipped mouthpiece, but it's much the same idea. Out of turbulence comes purity. Treated in the right way, a simple orifice will yield hidden delights. Isn't that gratifyingly natural and mysterious? Remember though – that pipe was once the body of a nymph. It's Syrinx we have to thank.

'The Sweetness o' the Man of Strings'

Since the twang of the first hunter's bow, strings have been plucked. That plucked string takes us back beyond the science of Pythagoras, to a mythic age of gods and heroes, to a time when, as Kipling put it, 'Omer smote 'is bloomin' lyre'. Back then, a tortoise-shell strung with gut was the instrument of choice for the neighbourhood bard as he launched into his latest saga. In Greek mythology, Orpheus, leader of the Muses and fount of all things arty, was the sweet singer and lyre-player who beguiled the fearsome guardians of the underworld into letting him pass. The story, enacted in the earliest operas, was recycled as recently as 1984, by Harrison Birtwistle in *The Mask of Orpheus*. St Cecilia may be music's sanitised patron of the Christian era, but Orpheus is its original pagan figurehead.

It's a small step from the ancient lyre to the harp in its basic form, as played by angels in stained glass. It's a larger step from this basic harp to the sophisticated gilt monster of the modern concert hall. Look closely at an orchestral harp, and you'll see it has seven pedals. Not pedals like those on a piano, nor like those on an organ, which are really just another keyboard. The seven pedals on a harp affect the tuning.

The player has to stretch towards the 'pillar' of the instrument to reach the deepest (longest) strings, while the highest (shortest) ones are close to the player's nose. Play all the notes of the harp from bottom to top, and you hear a major scale, like playing only the white notes of the piano. To be accurate, they are tuned a semitone lower, so what you hear is a scale of C♭ major. To get the 'black notes', pedals are brought into play. Press one pedal, and all the C♭s will be raised a semitone to become Cs. Press another, and all the D♭s will go up to Ds. Another raises the E♭s, and so on. Set all seven pedals in the down position, using the available notches to hold them there, and the harp's normal scale of C♭ becomes a scale of C. There's a second, lower notch for the pedals too. With a pedal in this lower position, the note affected will be raised two semitones. The C ♭ s, for example, will become C#s, now sounding at the same pitch as the adjacent D ♭ string.

Harpists have to play more glissandos, or slides, than anyone else. On the piano, it's easily done upwards with the back of the fingers, or downwards with a thumbnail, using your right hand. Even non-pianists – especially non-pianists! – find it hard to resist a quick glissando when they see a defenceless keyboard. The piano music of the matinee idol Franz Liszt legitimised this vulgar trick long ago. His *Mephisto Waltz* has a flashy double-handed glissando in octaves, on the white notes of course. Balakirev's *Oriental Fantasy*, *Islamey*, once regarded as the most difficult piano piece ever, goes one better, with a rising octave glissando to be spanned by right hand alone!

Even he was beaten to it by Beethoven, who wrote descending octave glissandos for the right hand in the *Piano Concerto No. 1* and in the *Waldstein Sonata*. Significantly, both pieces are in C. With the other hand busy elsewhere, no cheating is possible. Ravel writes a soft double glissando in parallel fourths for right hand alone – *Alborada del Gracioso*, from the suite *Miroirs* – perhaps made easier by the shallow touch of the composer's French Erard piano. Well, that's one excuse for those of us who can't play it. Manuel de Falla, in his sultry *Nights in the Gardens of Spain*, asks for a loud glissando on black notes – rather painful, but mercifully covered by the orchestra – and the normally reticent Debussy demands, in his *Feux d'artifice* (*Fireworks*), a truly pyrotechnical two-handed glissando on white and black notes simultaneously. Ouch! Thus, the second book of preludes ends with a bang, followed by the whimper of a distant *Marseillaise*. It is a French firework display, after all.

Apartheid still rules in piano music. A single-handed glissando can be black, or it can be white, but not a mixture of both. The beauty of harp glissandos is that almost any permutation of seven different notes per octave can be set up by the pedal positions, including reiterated, enharmonic notes like C# and D ♭ , which, though different in notation, are the same in pitch. Once the appropriate pedals are set, a glissando of stunning complexity can be played with a graceful sweep of the arm. One reason why female harpists (for they still are, mostly) should have lovely arms. Until quite recently, certain great orchestras had a men-only rule, with the exception of harpists, whose presence among all the black suits was, in the words of the composer Ethel Smyth, like 'a flower on a coal dump'. Even more astonishing effects can be achieved with two or three harps – Wagner uses six in the *Ring Cycle* – each with a different pedal setting. But with harp glissandos, the law of diminishing returns kicks in. In romantic film scores, the upbeat swirl of the harp as the orchestra reaches another emotional peak is now a well-worn cliché.

Fingers and arms are helpful adjuncts in harp playing, but early practitioners found that when the instrument was hung aloft, perhaps in a nearby tree during a lunch break, playful zephyrs got to work. Perfect for the non-musician, or for the merely lazy, this is the Aeolian harp, activated by the wind. The biblical King David, no mean harpist himself, tells us in *Psalm 137* that the exiled Israelites hung their harps on willows. This was not so much a musical experiment as a downing of tools. They would not play to their captors in a strange land. The true, zephyr-powered Aeolian harp, an ancestor of the wind chimes of suburbia, has a natural charm offset by the essentially random and open-ended nature of its performance, as modern-day neighbours will testify. It is essentially low-tech. Something comparable may be obtained from a rotary clothes dryer in a gale.

The radical American composer Henry Cowell, who died in 1965, was fascinated by musical randomness, though, oddly enough, his piano miniature *Aeolian Harp* is anything but random. Briefly the teacher of George Gershwin, he was also a friend and biographer of that other great American radical, Charles Ives. Cowell spent four years in prison convicted of homosexuality on the evidence of a young blackmailer, but continued with his avant-garde composing, laying the foundations for the work of John Cage. *Aeolian Harp* consists of a series of simple, one-handed chords, notated in the conventional way. The pianist silently fingers these chords, taking care to make no sound, while he leans forward and, with the other hand, gently strums the strings of the piano. A grand piano is essential, and I have found that a credit card makes the perfect plectrum. So long as the chosen notes are held down, the undamped strings will vibrate, each chord blending seamlessly, one hopes, into the next, without the characteristic sound of the hammer-strike. Eerily beautiful it is too.

Of the huge family of strummers and pluckers, some members are more ubiquitous than others. There is the guitar, which attained great popularity in nineteenth-century Spain, where it was thrashed in fiery flamenco, and caressed in neo-baroque studies. Since the birth of rock 'n' roll, it has conquered the world. The three simple guitar chords which anchored the blues in the Mississippi Delta were unleashed, horribly amplified, on white European suburbs by spotty adolescents.

In a quieter age, the melancholy of Tudor England found its perfect expression in the lute, the guitar's refined elderly relative. But elderly relatives can surprise us. If you think the rock guitar is a phallic symbol, take a look at the *chittarone*, or bass lute. On a smaller scale there is the tinny mandolin, ideal for serenading, as in Mozart's *Don Giovanni*, also used in Mahler's *Das Lied von der Erde*, and making a dazzling show in Act II of Prokoviev's *Romeo and Juliet*. Hummel, a contemporary of Beethoven, even wrote a concerto for it. And who would have expected such a modest instrument to star in a novel and a film, as in *Captain Corelli's Mandolin*? But it should not get above itself. Remember the bouzouki and *Zorba the Greek*? After its few minutes in the showbiz spotlight, it returned to its place in the Greek sun.

The triangular balalaika was twanged en masse by the all-singing, all-dancing Red Army ensemble, the Soviet Union's scariest cultural export during the Cold War. The wiry plonking of the banjo, for ever an American hillbilly sound, was mimicked in a nineteenth-century piano showpiece, *The Banjo*, by Louis Gottschalk, the USA's answer to Franz Liszt. Debussy paid his own tribute, *Minstrels*, in a pastel-shaded French way. And where would the toothy grin, the winks and the double-entendres of George Formby have taken him without his little ukulele in his hand?

All the aforementioned have their own peculiar body-shapes (the instruments, not the players), giving each its special identity.

The lute, looking like a laterally sliced pear, has often been posed in still-life paintings alongside ripe fruit. To Picasso, the guitar's more feminine contours were endlessly appealing. Whatever its shape, the body is there for resonance. Sometimes sets of strings were stretched more mundanely in a horizontal box-frame and played with mallets, like the dulcimer or psaltery of the mediaeval era. Not dissimilar is the Hungarian zither, or *cimbalom*, which stepped out of the East European folk band and into the concert hall for Kodaly's colourful *Háry János* music. Then, a couple of decades later, the zither made another surprise appearance, this time in the sewers of Vienna. Anton Karas's score for the film *The Third Man* caught the public imagination with its jaunty but faintly sinister air.

So much for plucking and hammering. But there are other ways to activate a string. When the bowing and scraping began is hard to say. The twelfth-century *tromba marina* was bowed, its single long string being touched at the nodal points, so as to produce only the natural harmonics, like the monochord of Pythagoras. The tone might have been a bit like a distant trumpet, hence the name *tromba*, but the nautical connection implied by *marina* is harder to explain. The mechanised hurdy-gurdy had its strings kept in motion by a wheel coated with resin, and cranked by a handle. Against this constant drone, you could finger a merry tune on a rudimentary keyboard with your free hand. A portable one-man band, ideal for minstrels.

The more formal family of viols thrived in the England of the Stuarts. Ranging in size from bass to tiny treble, they were all held between the knees and played like a cello. With no spike to give support, one needed naturally prehensile knees. Unlike the modern string family, the viols usually had six strings, fretted fingerboards like a guitar, and elegant sloping shoulders not unlike the modern double bass. Bowing was performed under-hand, and one finger regulated the tautness of the bow-hair. To play in a consort of viols was to partake in a dialogue among equals, each thread of melody woven into the texture to create the whole tapestry. In seventeenth-century England, this civilised pursuit lived on borrowed time, while in Italy the violin began to take centre stage.

The new instrument offered a dashing mix of sweetness and brilliance. Perfect in the role of soloist with small orchestra, it became the chief spokesman of baroque music, capable of great tenderness, yet forceful and dazzling when need be. Its popularity shows no sign of abating, as *The Four Seasons* bursts for the umpteenth time on to CD. In the hands of Vivaldi, reluctant priest and fiddler extraordinaire, the violin's top string, E, scaled dizzying heights, demanding ever more frenzied fingerwork, ever more carrying power. In his footsteps came other composing violinists, mainly from Italy, and a new breed was born – the travelling virtuoso.

The violin, with its dashing, seductive character, has long been the chosen instrument of Lucifer. As Shakespeare's Falstaff remarks, 'The Devil rides upon a fiddle-stick'. Somehow a sedentary Satan crouched over a cello would be less convincing. In about 1714, the Italian violinist-composer Giuseppe Tartini dreamed that the Devil borrowed his violin and played the most ravishing solo on it. On waking, he found the music past recall, but the *Devil's Trill Sonata* was the closest he could get. Later, in the over-heated Romantic imagination, the violin was still keeping bad company. It found its way into solo piano pieces. *The Mephisto Waltz* of Liszt, himself a purveyor of demonic virtuosity, draws on a version of the Faust story, in which Mephistopheles takes Faust to a village wedding, plays his violin and steals the bride. The orchestral *Danse Macabre*, by Saint-Saëns, showcases the Devil (in practice the leader of the orchestra) noisily tuning his fiddle, before leading the undead in a graveyard hoedown. And despite the violin's unsavoury reputation, some people never learn, do they? In *The Soldier's Tale*, Stravinsky's acerbic theatre piece of 1917, a soldier unwisely barters his violin with a mysterious stranger. Anyone inhabiting a Russian folk tale ought to have known that the fiddling stranger would be Old Nick himself.

A distinct whiff of sulphur hung about the cadaverous figure of Niccolo Paganini, still the most celebrated violinist of all time, though he died long ago, in 1840. He did nothing to discourage his Mephistophelean image, appearing on stage in a tight-fitting black outfit, his lank hair hanging around his shoulders. Being a shrewd businessman, he declined to begin until he was safely in possession of his share of the night's takings, which he usually stashed in a box between his feet as he played the first item. He also played the guitar, and as a viola player commissioned a concerto from Berlioz, another guitarist. The result, *Harold in Italy*, was not showy enough for him, but having heard it he was won over and paid Berlioz 20,000 francs a few days later.

In Thomas Hardy's novel *Under the Greenwood Tree*, members of the old church gallery band, string players to a man, agree that other instruments may have their place but the fiddle reigns supreme. 'If you'd thrive in musical religion', says one, 'stick to strings'. Another one voices a suspicion, in a broad Wessex accent, of course, that it may have a darker side: 'There's always a rakish, scampish twist about a fiddle's looks that seems to say the Wicked One had a hand in making o'en.' You can see his point. Folk tales are full of itinerant fiddlers, and, like the Dark Fiddler in Delius's opera *A Village Romeo and Juliet*, they are usually up to no good. Sometimes they come to a sticky end. To this day the English countryside is dotted with standing stones which are really petrified violinists, turned to stone for the sin of playing dance tunes on the Sabbath.

All stringed instruments have a standard tuning at which they function best. Even so, boundaries are there to be pushed. Scordatura is the fancy name for tinkering with this tuning. Guitarists regularly drop the pitch of their lowest string for ease of access to certain keys. Schumann does something similar to the cello in his *Piano Quartet*. In Stravinsky's *The Rite of Spring* the entire cello section detunes the top string, A, down to G# in the penultimate bar, so as to make the final chord playable. This deregulated chord, played by all the cellos on all four strings together – insofar as four strings arranged in an arc can be played together – is part of the leaden thump marking the end of the work. One would hardly notice if it was out of tune, and it probably is. Stravinsky could have scored it more conventionally, but in 1913, he was packing in every gimmick he could think of.

Common enough on the guitar, scordatura is rare on the violin. It was used by the seventeenth-century violinist and composer Heinrich Biber, whose vividly descriptive solo sonatas are seeing a welcome revival. A better-known example is Mahler's

Fourth Symphony, where the leader of the orchestra takes out a specially prepared violin – he certainly won't use his precious Stradivarius – with all four strings tuned up a whole tone, to convey the scratchy sound of a cheap fiddle. Needless to say, it's our old friend the Mahlerian *Dance of Death*. More surprisingly, no one listening in the eighteenth-century to Mozart's delightfully euphonious *Sinfonia Concertante* would have guessed that, while the solo violin part is written in the key of E♭, the solo viola is reading his own part in D, a semitone lower. Why? Because Mozart wanted the instrument tuned a semitone sharper than normal. Fingered in D, the music would sound in E♭ to match the other players, but the tauter strings would create a more equal partnership with the violin.

As a piece of craftwork, a certain mystique is attached to the violin. Not to mention value. Even bows can be worth a small fortune. A handful of names, particularly the elite Italian makers of Cremona – Guarnerius, Amati, Stradivarius – still cause a flutter in auction rooms around the world. So what's the magic ingredient? Musicians and scientists are baffled. Among the myriad explanations for the unique tone-quality of these instruments, a recent favourite was the presence of volcanic ash in the varnish. Mmm, well, maybe... But could it all just be in the mind? Experts have undergone blind tests, where a modern Japanese stainless steel violin has been preferred to a fine antique from Cremona. So it's not certain that any magic ingredients exist. Still, if you stumble over a dusty violin in your attic with the monogram of a Maltese cross and the initials A S (Antonio Stradivari) inside a double circle, it might just be worth checking.

Haydn, Mozart and Beethoven all played the violin, though Mozart had a preference for the deeper, elegiac tone of the viola. All wrote for the string quartet too, that self-sufficient and perfectly balanced foursome which is the hallmark of the classical style. And by 1800 the modern orchestra had arrived. The various off-the-peg ensembles of the baroque era, when composers wrote chiefly for what was available, had settled into the more regular groupings of the string-centred classical orchestra, the basis of what we know today.

In time, the exclusively string orchestra found a special place in people's affections. And what a remarkable emotional range it commands! From the sparkle of Mozart's *Eine Kleine Nachtsmusik*, through the lush serenades of Dvorak and Tchaikovsky, to the *Introduction and Allegro* of Elgar, the *Tallis Fantasia* of Vaughan Williams, and further still into the searing sound-world of Bernard Hermann's 1960 *Psycho* score, or Penderecki's *Threnody for the Victims of Hiroshima*, the string orchestra's unique richness and depth has inspired the very best from first-rate composers. And its repertoire is singularly non-transferable. After all, leaving aside the aberration of a choral arrangement by the composer himself, who can seriously imagine the *Adagio* of Samuel Barber played by anything but strings?

The violin, unlike its more staid colleagues the viola, cello and double bass, has been a key player on the folk scene too, with an endless store of laments, jigs and reels for every occasion. Thomas Hardy, raised in a rustic family of amateur musicians, was a keen folk-fiddler himself. He loved nothing more than to play for local dances, and one of those grumbling church band members from *Under the Greenwood Tree* sums things up with a splendid finality:

> Your brass-man is a rafting [rousing] dog – well and good; your reed-man is a dab at stirring ye – well and good; your drum-man is a rare bowel-shaker – good again. But I don't care who hears me say it, nothing will spak to your heart wi' the sweetness o' the man of strings.

And, pausing just long enough to acknowledge that many of today's finest string players are in fact women, who will argue with that?

Keyboards from Byrd...

The harpsichord is really a harp turned on its side and put in a box. The action of the player's arms and fingers has been mechanised by adding levers – keys – each of which operates a plectrum, originally made of goose-quill, but probably nylon now. The player, one step removed from the strings, sits with hands poised over a horizontal keyboard – or two in the case of the larger instruments. These keyboards, or manuals, are connected to different sets of strings, each with its own tone-quality. The connection is made by drawing stops or moving levers, or possibly by operating foot-pedals, which can be notched in the down position. An extra set of strings, tuned an octave higher, may be coupled to the regular strings so that every note is duplicated in octaves for greater power. There may also be an auxiliary set of strings, brought into play by a 'buff' stop, giving a delicate lute-like sound.

Not everyone loves the harpsichord. Someone once described its characteristic jangle as sounding like a birdcage played with a toasting fork. You can appreciate what they meant. But anyone who doubts its primal rhythmic energy should listen to the first movement of Bach's *Brandenburg Concerto No. 5*, where the harpsichordist begins as a demure support act, part of the traditional cello-keyboard team known as the *basso continuo*, but then grows in brilliance and complexity, until finally it stuns the other instruments into silence and embarks on a whirlwind solo fantasia.

Not everyone could afford or accommodate a full-size harpsichord, so makers offered a range of sizes and designs. The full-size version was roughly triangular, like a small, squared-off grand piano. The spinet, like its close relative the virginals, was built like a rectangular box with the strings running across in front of the player. Unlike the modern piano, whose gleaming black surface is relieved only by the maker's name, the harpsichord was often decorated with pastoral scenes, inlaid with coloured woods, and emblazoned with an improving motto in Latin. The finest examples, usually from Antwerp, combined all that was best in woodwork, furniture making and instrumental technology.

English musicians of the Elizabethan period excelled in the writing and performance of harpsichord music. In the early seventeenth century hundreds of pieces were gathered into collections such as *Parthenia*, *My Lady Nevell's Booke*, and the *Fitzwilliam Virginal Book*. Despite many skilled male players like John Bull – as famous, according to the then Archbishop of Canterbury, for 'marring of the virginity as for fingering of virginals' – the instrument never lost its feminine character. This was nothing to do with Elizabeth herself, though. The name virginals long predated the time when the queen had, like Doris Day, become a virgin, and it was well after her death that the 1611 collection *Parthenia* ('Virginity' to those cultivated Elizabethans who knew Greek) was announced as the 'maidenhead of the first music that ever was printed for the virginals'.

The name of William Byrd figures prominently in these collections, not surprising when you consider the twenty-one year monopoly on the printing of music granted to him and his teacher Thomas Tallis by their musical monarch. The home keyboard fed the appetite for popular dance-tunes, and the Sunday-afternoon harpsichordist had an endless supply of pavanes, galliards and almans, many with fancy variations added. If he wished to stir his dancing womenfolk into something more energetic, the new *La Volta* from those saucy Italians might elicit that same little ankle-revealing leap with which Elizabeth delighted her court. And, so long as the Protestant Elizabeth frisked to the latest tunes arranged by William Byrd, his (Roman Catholic) head would remain attached to his shoulders. Happily, and somewhat surprisingly, it stayed in place for eighty years.

Nowadays, many regard the harpsichord as a somewhat bland forerunner of the more colourful piano. In its time, though, it was a vehicle for musical fantasy, some pieces giving a blow-for-blow commentary on a battle, or on the weather. The Elizabethan taste for whimsical titles – *The Fall of the Leafe*, *Farnaby's Dream*, *Doctor Bulls Myselfe*, *My Lady Carey's Dumpe*, *The Woodes So Wilde* –

extended also to the golden era of the French clavecinistes. Look out for Couperin's *Le moucheron*, which depicts the monotonous buzzing of a gnat as only a harpsichord can. This gnat is a precursor of the insect made famous in Bartok's piano miniature, *From the Diary of a Fly*. Though written for two different keyboards, and separated by over 200 years, these two should get together: Hungarian fly seeks French gnat with a view to two-part counterpoint.

The harpsichord was more than just a vehicle for the playing of charming trifles, and, in the later baroque period, profound and complex thoughts were entrusted to the instrument, like Bach's *48 Preludes and Fugues*. Important as they are, however, Bach's celebrated '48' are a disparate bunch, some of which are better suited to a small chamber organ, or to the clavichord, of which more later.

Perhaps the Everest of harpsichord music is the extraordinary *Goldberg Variations*. Bach's thirty variations on his own *Sarabande* theme – played at the beginning and at the end – show the rich variety with which melodic lines can be combined while still adhering to the same harmonic foundation. Here are canons to the right of us and canons to the left of us, one melody following its twin after a few beats time-lag. When the pitch of the melodies is the same, it is a canon at the unison, the commonest type. Examples crop up in later music, when Romantic composers want to show off their academic credentials – the march from Bizet's *L'Arlesienne*, the slow movement of Borodin's *2nd String Quartet* (shamelessly plundered for the musical Kismet), and the cunning game of tag between violin and piano in the finale of the famous *Franck Sonata* (not to be confused with the famous Frank Sinatra).

Bach could write several such canons before breakfast. And the *Goldberg Variations* goes further. The melodies, complex in themselves, and often changing key as they go, are fitted together at nine different pitch relationships. After one canon at the unison (*Variation 3*) there is one at the second (*Variation 6*) – that's to say the melody follows its twin, one step higher in pitch – one at the third (*Variation 9*), one at the fourth (*Variation 12*), one at the fifth (*Variation 15*), and so on up to an octave. The final canon (*Variation 27*) is a canon at the ninth – an octave plus one step –

then he calls it a day. Each time, the melodic partners in the canon mesh together over a moving bass-line in such a way that the resulting harmony broadly matches the chords under the original theme.

Imagine a crudely equivalent process in speech, much easier to follow with everything reduced to a simple rhythmic monotone. Try reading aloud, with a strongly marked rhythm, the verse on the opposite page, and get someone else to read the same verse, but starting four beats later. You may have to beat time to keep together. In the background, by the way, someone else is reciting a different poem entirely. That's the bass-line.

Voice 2, having started last, will be the last to finish, with a few cheap tin trays left over. In the musical version, a composer will usually trim the last few notes of the trailing voice so that everyone reaches the finishing-line together.

You could go on if you're enjoying yourself. See the works of John Masefield, sailor and poet laureate, for more of these salty stanzas, though anything rhythmic will do. Some people find rhythms everywhere. I know of one small child – my father, in fact – who would stand with his sister in the Edgware Road, and take great delight in chanting aloud the sign over a shop: EVERYTHING ELECTRICAL: ELECTRIC LIGHTING, HEATING, MOTORS, BELLS AND PHONES.

For the more ambitious, there's a real piece by Ernst Toch called *Geographical Fugue*. Made up entirely of place names recited in rhythm, quite tongue-twisting in places, but with no pitched sounds at all, it would suit a group of singers who can't sing. They must, however, have a sense of rhythm and will need someone who can read music to direct operations.

In the *Goldberg Variations*, Bach, the one-man canon factory, interleaves these little miracles with other baroque styles, some of the livelier ones making full use of the two manuals of the harpsichord. Since the keyboard here is used primarily for the working out of musical challenges, and not so much for its tonal colour, the work can be played quite successfully on a modern piano. With only one keyboard, though, the positions of the player's hands need careful planning – right over left or left over right? – to avoid them becoming inextricably knotted together.

Beats	1	2	3	4	5	6	7	8
Voice 1:	Dirty	British	coaster	with a	salt-	caked	smoke-	stack
Voice 2:	—	—	—	—	Dirty	British	coaster	with a
Voice 3:	Some are	fond of	red	wine and	some are	fond of	white,	And

Beats	1	2	3	4	5	6	7	8
Voice 1:	Butting	through the	Channel	in the	mad	March	days	With a
Voice 2:	Salt-	caked	smoke-	stack	Butting	through the	Channel	in the
Voice 3:	some are	all for	dancing	by the	pale	moon-	light...	But

Beats	1	2	3	4	5	6	7	8
Voice 1:	car-	go of	Tyne	coal,	Road-	rail,	pig-	lead
Voice 2:	mad	March	days	With a	car-	go of	Tyne	coal,
Voice 3:	rum a-	lone's the	tipple,	and the	heart's	de-	light	Of the

Beats	1	2	3	4	5	6	7	8
Voice 1:	Fire-	wood,	iron-	ware and	cheap	tin	trays.	—
Voice 2:	Road-	rail,	pig-	lead	Fire-	wood,	iron-	ware and
Voice 3:	old	bold	mate of	Henry	Mor-	gan.	—	—

So, will you actually hear all this wondrous contrapuntal ingenuity? Probably not, or not much of it anyway, but what fun you
will have trying! Repeated hearings will reveal more of what is
going on but, as with so much good music, it's a mixture of
hearing and understanding, part ear and part brain. Just knowing
about it is a start. The work is said to have been commissioned by
a chronic insomniac, not, presumably, as a form of sleeping-
draught – unconsciousness is not the ideal condition in which to
appreciate Bach, after all – but as an intellectual stimulus during
hours of unnatural wakefulness.

The harpsichord's pre-eminence waned towards the end of
the eighteenth century. When the Wunderkind Mozart astonished
the courts of Europe, it was a harpsichord he played on. In
adulthood he performed his concertos on the piano, or an early
form of it anyway. But the harpsichord had enjoyed a long and
productive career. Both as a solo instrument and as the harmonic
'glue' in ensembles, it had been indispensable for about 300 years.
The piano has yet to attain such longevity.

...to Cage

When Bach was still a teenager, the instrument-maker Bartolomeo Cristofori was busy turning out harpsichords in his Florence workshop. Having a spare afternoon, he decided to replace the quill mechanism of a harpsichord with tiny hammers, so that the strings were struck rather than plucked. His plan was simple but far-reaching. The harder you struck the key, the louder the sound. Though small by modern standards, a gradation of volume was possible. The keyboard action was what we would now call 'touch-sensitive'. This individual control of each note, Cristofori realised, would open up new expressive scope. In 1700, he patented the invention under the catchy name of *clavicembalo col piano e forte*, a harpsichord with soft and loud, but the idea failed to impress, and although he tinkered with it for the rest of his life he never saw the rich harvest that this seed would yield.

Early pianos retained the squared-off wing-shape of the harpsichord. Smaller and weaker in tone than the modern grand piano, their compass was only a few octaves, and to the casual modern listener the sound hardly differs from that of a harpsichord. But if it was slow to get started, the piano, or *Hammerklavier* in German, was an idea whose time had come, and instrument makers set to work. Finally, in the 1760s, it began to make an impact on the musical world. After the initial scepticism of J S Bach, his son C P E Bach, a harpsichordist by training, wrote some of the earliest piano sonatas, while his much younger son, J C Bach, became the piano's most avid exponent in his regular London concerts. In 1774, the eight-year-old Mozart paid him a visit, and they played duets together. Mozart never forgot the kindness shown to him on that occasion, and later wove a J C Bach phrase into his *Piano Concerto No. 12* as a token of homage when he heard of the older composer's death.

A German company popularised the so-called 'square piano', a compact box-shape like the old spinet, with strings running parallel to the keyboard. The English square piano, made by Broadwood, would have responded to the manicured fingers of Jane Austen's heroines. One large Broadwood grand, of modern shape, and suitably reinforced, was dispatched to Vienna as a gift to Beethoven, whose treatment of pianos grew rougher as his hearing deteriorated. The composer Spohr, who knew Beethoven, reports how, at a concert in 1808, the audience was reduced to hysterics as the enraged composer, dissatisfied with the performance, struck a chord with such force that he broke six strings!

The internal action of the piano underwent constant refinement, partly as a defence against such brutality, and partly in a search for sustaining power and sweetness of tone. In America, the upright model was introduced as a space-saving convenience. Touch became lighter, and more responsive. Special thought was given to ways in which the vibrating string could be efficiently damped. With the wooden frame replaced by an iron one, the strings – grouped three to a note in the middle register – could be put under extreme tension, the stress being distributed more evenly by over-stringing – one set of strings passing diagonally over another.

The sustaining – right-hand side – pedal raised all dampers at once, and allowed the sound to ring on after the note had been released. The soft – left-hand side – pedal thinned the tone by causing the hammers to move a little to one side, and strike only one string per note, an effect notated in the music as *una corda* – one string. In the 1870s, the New York firm of Steinway developed the ingenious sostenuto – middle – pedal that enabled only the last-selected note(s) to ring on undamped. Imagine a chord held on by this middle pedal, while both hands are free to play crisp, detached chords over the top of it – a vital resource for composers like Debussy. Piano manufacturers still regard this as a special feature, reserved for classier models, and it should not be confused with that other middle pedal commonly found on modern uprights, which by muting the sound to almost nothing allows you to practise at three in the morning without complaints from the neighbours.

Today the piano, often rudely elbowed aside by its tarty younger sister, the electronic keyboard, is here to stay. All over the world – in homes, schools, hotels, village halls, churches, pubs, clubs and bars – it stands defiant. Sometimes in sulky dereliction, with stuck keys and moth-eaten felts, often in semi-neglected gentility, rattled into life by a reluctant child, but occasionally – and inspiringly – in gleaming pristine splendour, awaiting the touch of an international virtuoso.

One of the most curious manifestations of piano technology was the player-piano, or, to give it its better-known trade-name, the pianola. In the 1920s, the USA produced more player-pianos than conventional ones. Looking like an upright piano, and usable as one, it was also a kind of low-tech record-player. The 'record', a roll of perforated paper, was inserted into the front of the instrument, and the pianist, who needed to be no such thing, pumped away at a pair of foot pedals. The air pressure provided life to the player-piano, which 'read' the perforations on the turning cylinder, and caused the appropriate keys to be pressed. Suddenly, on your parlour piano, Rachmaninov was playing his arrangement of the *Flight of the Bumble Bee* – and the faster you pumped, the faster he played. The effect could be stunning, though even your myopic granny would not be deluded into thinking you had improved that much.

Seen by some as an amusing novelty, the pianola and its vast store of surviving piano rolls have acquired greater significance with the passing of time. Recordings made by such luminaries as Debussy, Mahler and Grainger throw light on historic performing styles. Stravinsky, temperamentally resistant to the mechanisation of music, admired the pianola's 'limitless possibilities of speed, precision and polyphony'.

Exploring these possibilities, the American, Mexico-domiciled composer Conlon Nancarrow made the creation of original piano-rolls his life's work. Since his death in 1997, his extraordinary *Studies for Player-Piano* have achieved almost cult status. Ranging from riotous boogie-woogie, to canons and fugues of staggering complexity, they have been copied on to computer and also recorded live on a piano, using multiple tracks where the brain and fingers of the finest pianists admit defeat. Nothing, though, quite matches the dry and rather comical sound-world of Nancarrow's own piano-rolls, home-made in his garage with a heavy, hand-operated punch, which after years of use gave him a right arm bicep of Popeye-proportions.

Though Nancarrow's studies mechanised the piano to a literally superhuman level of speed and co-ordination, it's still a piano, and we hear the pitches of its eighty-eight notes intact. John Cage took a different approach. He had heard his teacher, Henry Cowell, playing directly on the piano strings – we met Cowell's *Aeolian Harp* earlier – using his fingers to pluck and mute them. In the 1940s, Cage began modifying the sounds of a (grand) piano by inserting objects into the strings, initially as a practical measure when the percussion instruments needed for a new dance piece proved too large to fit into the performing space available. Each of Cage's 'prepared piano' scores begins with its own 'table of preparations', listing the nature and size of the required object – screw, nut, bolt, eraser – and the exact position where it must be wedged between the strings.

The effect is enchanting. Not only is the pitch of each 'prepared' note changed out of recognition, so that playing a scale becomes as indeterminate as running a stick along park-railings – though more beautiful – the tone-quality bears little relation to that of a piano. Some notes have their harmonics magically isolated; some blossom into tiny chords; some take on the sound of miniature gongs or drums. This delicately oriental sound, evoking the traditional Indonesian percussion ensemble, or gamelan, reflected Cage's disenchantment with what he saw as the coarse music of the West.

Many a mainstream music lover, having warmed to a recording of a Cage prepared piano – 'such a lovely reminder of the holiday we spent in Bali, darling' – is convulsed with rage on discovering how the sounds are made. 'Foreign objects stuck inside the piano? But that's ridiculous! Was he mad?'

So how do we define this maverick musician? An eccentric? Certainly. A visionary? Yes, in a way. A philosopher too. And an acknowledged expert on mushrooms and fungi – yes, really! Schoenberg, another of his teachers, described him as more of an inventor than a composer. Look out for his *Sonatas and Interludes for Prepared Piano*, and judge for yourself.

I've saved till last the most reticent of keyboard instruments, which, first referred to about 1400, inhabits a world of Cage-like delicacy.

The clavichord is housed in a rectangular case just like the virginals, and the strings run lengthways, braced over a wooden bridge. As in all keyboard instruments, each key pivots on a fulcrum like a seesaw, but there is no hammer for striking, no quill for plucking. In the clavichord, the end farthest from the player is fitted with a thin brass plate called a tangent. The tangent comes up to strike the string with its edge, but does not fall back like the hammer in a piano. Instead, it stays in contact with the string for as long as the player keeps his finger pressed down, even permitting a little tasteful vibrato by wobbling the key.

So how does the string vibrate if a brass plate is pressing against it? Amazingly, the tangent strikes and sets resonating that part of the string it has just marked off, the pitch of the note fixed by the distance between tangent and bridge. And why doesn't the rest of the string vibrate as well? Good question. It's because the rest of the string is muted by a piece of cloth, that's why! Heath Robinson couldn't have managed it better.

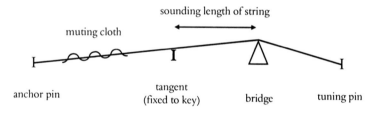

You may have spotted from this that a clavichord could make do with just one string, so long as you only played one note at a time. The tangents could all touch the same string in different places, though it would get a bit crowded with the higher notes. In theory it's possible, and in the seventeenth century there were often fewer strings than keys. Several notes on the keyboard, the ones least likely to be played together, would share the same string.

With its endearing blend of economy and simplicity, the clavichord was the Renault Five of the keyboard world. Since the time of Mozart, it's been on the endangered list, if not wholly extinct.

The early music business has thrown it a lifeline, however, and you can be sure someone somewhere is at this very minute poring over the plans for a homemade kit version. One last thing should be mentioned. To say it is quiet is an understatement. It's almost inaudible. In Bohemia, the eighteenth-century music historian Charles Burney came across a whole roomful of clavichordists all practising away on different pieces without bothering each other. Young Handel, forbidden by his father from pursuing the worthless profession of music, is said to have crept by night to the attic, where he practised undetected on an old clavichord.

Bach loved it too, and some of his music, printed with the unspecific label '*Klavier*', or keyboard, suits the clavichord better than the harpsichord or organ. In practical terms, though, a clavichord recital, if one can imagine such a thing, would have the audience craning forward, whispering, 'Has it started yet?' As for amplification, don't even think about it. It would make as much sense as looking at a bonsai tree through a magnifying glass. The sound of the clavichord is by definition faint, equivalent to a group of gnats playing hand-bells several miles away. That's just the way it is. Too quiet, perhaps, for the noisy modern world.

III
Intermezzo

Making Your Mark

Enjoying music is easy. Understanding it is harder. Why should composers give away their secrets like free-gift vouchers? But music, the argument goes, is a language, and the prime function of language is to communicate as clearly as possible. At times, yes, but language does more than just write letters or record information. It is more than a bank manager or an accountant. It is an acrobat, a juggler, a dancer. Language is for communicating, of course, but it's also for joking, and teasing, and punning, and deceiving. It's for irony, riddles, codes, secrets, and much else besides.

When Guillaume de Machaut worked as a canon at Rheims cathedral, in the fourteenth century, he would have been perfectly aware that the subtleties of his music were above the heads of the populace at large. Do you remember the *chanson* with the catchy title – *Ma fin est mon commencement et mon commencement ma fin* – in which one entire voice-part is a backwards version of another, and the third voice is symmetrical about a central point?

Notational advances in the *Ars Nova* (New Art) period allowed composers greater imaginative scope, but such abstract delights were accessible only to the initiated. Machaut would have been content with that. In the devout Middle Ages, the serious artist communed as much with God as with his fellow men and women. That communion represented spiritual credit in the heavenly bank. Why else would a stonemason devote a large portion of his life to work a hundred feet above ground level? Probing historians of the future might stumble across a mason's mark carved into the stone, but otherwise the man's identity is for ever lost – the work of his hands and his brain, a literal example of high art, visible only to a passing pigeon or jackdaw.

In Machaut's case, by the way, I like to think that those jackdaws were relatives of the famous Jackdaw of Rheims, immortalised by Richard Barham in his *Ingoldsby Legends* (1840), who stole the turquoise ring of the Cardinal Lord Archbishop, and was roundly cursed for it. All ends happily, however, when the reformed bird dies and is made a saint.

When that bold jackdaw, ring in beak perhaps, peered down at the microscopic figure of our musical cryptographer making its way across the cathedral precinct in Rheims, the world of the arts was a simpler place. The function of music in everyday life was one of entertainment or celebration. Its natural companion was dancing. High art, on the other hand, was the preserve of the trained intellectual. Real music was more than just a spontaneous effusion of feeling, played, or sung, by someone who had a natural talent for it. It was an art, and a craft, and a science. The touchy-feely approach of today's music education would, for all its vaunted inclusivity, have been regarded as shoddy in the extreme.

The mediaeval syllabus fell into two segments. Arithmetic, music, geometry and astronomy formed the higher division, or *quadrivium*. The *trivium*, or lower division, included grammar, rhetoric and logic. Clearly, no one would have maintained that a knowledge of theory alone would guarantee to turn you, say, into a brilliant lutenist, any more than a study of the laws of gravity will make you an Olympic high jumper. But a solid grounding in the science of music was essential to the true musician.

Because literacy was largely confined to the priesthood, it tended to be sacred music that survived, kept in ecclesiastical libraries over many centuries, often to the present day. So strongly did the tide run in the church's direction that when, for example, in the thirteenth century, an anonymous and probably secular musician wrote the complex six-voice canon, or round, *Summer is icumen in*, someone somewhere, also anonymous, felt that the rather earthy tone should be purified. The bucolic words, which welcome the new season, mention with disarming candour the methane-provoking effects of spring grass on animals, giving a fresh slant to the phrase *Ars Nova*.

'*Bullock sterteth, bucke verteth, murrie sing cu-cu*' – don't ask!

Such coarseness was thought unworthy of the high level of musical inspiration, and a more upmarket text, in Latin, of course, was supplied, expressing suitably pious religious sentiments.

As time went on, and God withdrew a little from human affairs, the composer craved a more personal relationship with his audience. More people played music from the written, or printed, note. Clear lines of communication were opened up. But still composers liked to keep something back.

One method of encoding secrets lay in the notes themselves. In our own time, many a young child has been encouraged in its piano-practice by puzzles and word-games. The fact that there are only seven notes named from A to G is a serious limitation and, so far as I know, C-A-B-B-A-G-E is the best anyone has done, not very promising when one aspires to the encryption of profundities. It would be nice to report that great strides were made, and that there are moments in Bach when the music spells out – in German, naturally – 'Down with the Pope' or 'Let's hear it for Martin Luther'.

The truth is more mundane. Certainly, German musical nomenclature is helped by the addition of two extra letters, H and S. The H denotes B (the letter B itself meaning B♭) and S is the useful name for E♭. But despite this, composers' messages have seldom risen higher than the 'Kilroy was here' variety. The Irish composer and pianist, John Field, a stout trencherman with a drink habit and a short fuse, wrote a musical thank-you note to a hostess who had fed him well. Not only does the word C-A-B-B-A-G-E appear in the tune, but there is some B-E-E-F to accompany it.

It is fitting that the greatest composer of all should be one of the few whose whole name can be spelled out in notes. B-A-C-H – or in English nomenclature B♭-A-C-B – yields quite a fertile little musical phrase. Bach himself used this neat monogram, and later composers paid homage by incorporating it into their own works. The arch-romantic, Franz Liszt, best known for his superhuman pianism, was also an organist (who says you can't do both?). His *Prelude and Fugue on the Name of Bach* draws from the organ the sort of torrential sound that would have had its baroque dedicatee running for cover.

In 1909, the altogether more fastidious Ravel paid tribute to Haydn with an elegant *Menuet sur le nom d'Haydn* for piano. The first five notes of the tune, labelled H-A-Y-D-N, are made available by Ravel's system of running the whole alphabet past the seven white notes as many times as it takes:

A	B	C	D	E	F	G
H	I	J	K	L	M	N
O	P	Q	R	S	T	U
V	W	X	Y	Z		

So, the note A serves also for H, O and V, and so on for the other notes. By this token, the tune should start with the same two notes, but Ravel reverts to the German method in making B (natural) stand for the letter H. The tune actually comes out as B-A-D-D-G. This centenary homage to Haydn is delivered in a sweetly-sour Parisian accent, yet with Ravel's precision and clarity one senses a real meeting of minds.

Robert Schumann was another of those composers mentioned earlier, who imagined they were taking dictation from a source outside themselves. In his case the ghost of Schubert sometimes did the honours. He was always a little odd, and that oddness sadly turned to something much more serious. To students of musical cryptography, though, Schumann is the king.

He started early with Opus 1, the *Abegg Variations* (1830), inspired, we are told, by Meta Abegg, a girl he had met at a ball. But Schumann was pulling our legs. Meta is simply an anagram of the Italian word *tema* (theme), and the piece takes the notes A-B♭-E-G-G as a starting-point for a rhapsodic set of variations. Look closely, and the lady vanishes.

Carnaval, another piano work by Schumann, is subtitled *Scènes mignonnes sur quatre notes* (dainty scenes on four notes). These notes, constantly juggled around, are A-S-C-H (that's A-E♭-C-B in non-German notation). Asch turns out to have been the home-town of his current flame, Ernestine von Fricken (yes, she was a real person), and, by a happy coincidence, these letters are the only ones in Schumann's own name capable of musical encryption: S-C-H-(um)-A-(nn).

Of its twenty-one movements, one is a real puzzle. Entitled *Sphinxes*, it consists of eleven single notes, various forms of A-S-C-H, played very slowly, unharmonised, and at a low pitch.

There is no division into bars, no time signature to suggest a pulse, and no indication of speed or volume. Each note appears as a breve, a square hollow note twice as long as a semibreve, almost obsolete in Schumann's time. No one has really explained the riddle, and in performance pianists often omit *Sphinxes*. The brooding Rachmaninov used to play them very slowly and very loudly in double octaves – but he would, wouldn't he?

The happiest time of Schumann's life was when he married the lovely Clara Wieck, a gifted pianist and composer in her own right. The story of their elopement, against her father's wishes, is the stuff of a Mills and Boon romance. How many prospective bridegrooms threaten to sue their future father-in-law for defamation? But Robert Schumann, unbalanced as he was, had read law at university, and knew what he was doing.

His one and only piano concerto, written for Clara to play, begins with a gentle theme made up of the notes C-H-A-A, a compressed version of 'Chiara', his Italianised pet name for her. The idyll was not to last. His behaviour became ever more erratic, and the asylum beckoned. With his encroaching madness, one imagines poor Schumann desperate to meet someone whose name or domicile would submit to the rigours of musical notation. Alas, he would never meet the German equivalent of that elusive Miss Cabbage, who might have crowned his crypto-graphical career. The best he could manage was a friendship with the rather underrated Danish composer, Niels Gade (pronounced 'Gairtha'). With what alacrity must he have rushed to the piano with a G-A-D-E theme already ringing in his head!

Brahms owed a great deal to the support and encouragement of the Schumanns, but whereas Robert Schumann had used the motto F-A-E in his music, standing for *Frei aber einsam* (free but lonely), Brahms modified this to F-A-F – *Frei aber froh* (free but happy). A lifelong bachelor, he adored Clara from a comfortable distance. As her long life transformed the girlish charm of her early portraits into the black-garbed widowhood of the photo-graphic era, Brahms was never far from her side, acting on her advice, revising and improving his works as she directed. He paid his final homage at her funeral in 1896, and followed her to the grave just months later.

With a name like Dmitri Shostakovich, the best advice might be, 'Don't even think about it.' But he did, and his musical monogram D-S-C-H crops up audibly in several works, notably the dark and introspective *String Quartet No. 8* (1960). For all its brevity, this innocuous little phrase conveys a real sense of anguish. The composer was on the brink of suicide, worn out by his cat-and-mouse game with the Soviet authorities, and deeply depressed by a recent visit to the bombed remains of Dresden. But wait a second! These four notes sound like D-E♭-C-B in English notation. We know that S stands for E♭ but where does that C come from? Well, some tinkering has been necessary. Russian names are rendered in the Cyrillic alphabet, so D-S-C-H actually derives from the German version, spelt 'Dimitri SCHostakowitch'. A tortuous solution, certainly, with most of the letters ignored. But such was his hankering for a hiding-place in the very fabric of his music.

Other examples show a lighter touch. In *Uranus the Magician*, the sixth movement of Holst's suite *The Planets*, the trombones announce the sorcerer in four solemn and powerful notes: G-E♭-A-B, or G-S-A-H in German notation. Fill in the blanks – quite a few – and you have GuStAv Holst. The trombone was Holst's own instrument, taken up to strengthen his weak chest and lungs. By encoding his own name in the magic spell, he makes himself the wizard. Music is magic, he tells us, and I, the composer, am in sole command of these mighty forces. A touch hubristic, one might think, but Holst was a modest chap, and this particular wizard is useless. For all his posturing, his spells go hopelessly wrong. Just listen to the explosive moment near the end. The huge orchestral sound includes a glissando, or slide, on the organ manuals, the sort of assault Jerry Lee Lewis's piano would undergo in the heyday of rock 'n' roll. An ominous silence follows. Then the music dwindles to nothing. The spell is a flop and in its collapse we hear the true, self-deprecating Holst.

Some musical ciphers have been more commercial. The Decca record company long advertised with a logo spelling the notes, D-E-C-C-A, on a little treble stave. To those who as children struggled through Associated Board instrumental grades, a five-note phrase such as this is chillingly reminiscent of that moment when the examiner stands the candidate out of sight of the keyboard and announces: 'Aural tests next! Please sing this melody, which I will play twice.'

But to anyone who saw the film *Close Encounters of the Third Kind*, Decca's musical logo now sounds like a slightly wrong version of the electronic signal played to welcome the alien craft, which lands like an illuminated wedding-cake in the final scene. D-E-C-C-G, hoots the earth-boffins' signal over and over again while the world holds its breath. (I confess to having transposed the tune into the notation-friendly key of C.) At last the aliens respond with a cheery greeting, supplying the last two notes themselves, with a blast somewhere between a giant intergalactic tuba and the *Queen Mary* docking at Southampton. D-E-C-C-G! Your puny earthling aural tests hold no terrors for us, they seem to say, and contact is made. But what might the Decca record company have paid them to blast C-A instead? Brainwashed by the kind of subliminal advertising that was briefly tried and banned, cinema-goers might have been puzzled to find themselves drawn to the record store on the way home.

The name of the Italian opera composer Giuseppe Verdi is fairly resistant to a musical interpretation, but it entered the political arena with a vengeance during his lifetime.

How fortunate for those chanting Italian crowds that their most beloved composer and their aspiring monarch should fit so neatly together. Their slogan, *'Vittorio Emanuele Re d'Italia!'* (Victor Emmanuel, King of Italy), was quickly turned into the less clumsy acronym V-E-R-D-I. *'Viva Verdi!'* they yelled, and everyone understood. No music needed.

And as for the famously mercenary Igor Stravinsky, a Russian composer transplanted to the USA, what deep Cold-War significance lies in those initials, superimposed to make a dollar-sign? Even the dour I S ($) must have allowed himself the faintest flicker of a smile as he lunched with the likes of Walt Disney, driving the hardest of commercial bargains, before returning to his composing desk.

For Your Eyes Only

Some aspects of music may be entirely visual. Unlike a painting, which will almost certainly have no aural dimension to its existence – you may hear the sound of bets being hedged here – a work of music almost always exists in both audible and visible mode. First and foremost, there is the performance: transient, fleeting, but giving real pleasure to the receptive listener, and demanding no specialist knowledge. For most people, this is the essence of the musical experience. But there is something else – the score. Leaving aside music that depends totally on improvisation, it is the written score that dictates everything we hear. And 'dictates' is not too strong a word, either. Performers may take certain prescribed liberties, but the overwhelming majority of decisions have already been taken and laid down by the composer. They are there to be obeyed.

A musical score, even of the simplest piece, uses a secret language full of mysterious symbols. But symbols, however mysterious, can be attractive in their own right. Think of Egyptian hieroglyphics, or Chinese calligraphy. And what could be more beautiful than cursive Arabic script? In the same way, a musician may look at a page of Stravinsky's *The Rite of Spring* – for me it's page 129 of the Boosey and Hawkes full score – block the mind to any musical response, and think what stunning wallpaper that would make!

Composers have always known this. Even in mediaeval times, scores might function on a visual level. Sometimes it was cosmetic, as when the initial letter of a sung text was painstakingly illuminated. Or it might reflect the sense of the words, especially when the music was directed primarily at the performers. In one fifteenth-century *chanson*, the vocal parts are complete in themselves, but some staves are left blank throughout, possibly to illustrate the subject of lost love. In the setting of a mass by the fifteenth-century Flemish composer Johannes Ockeghem, the notes turn black when we reach the Latin word *mortuorum* (of the dead). An Italian song of the period has a similar outbreak of black notes, when a peasant laments the death of his donkey. Aah! Musicologists have helpfully named this *augenmusik*, or eye-music.

Augenmusik was a particular feature of madrigals, where words like 'death', 'darkness', 'shade', 'night' were common currency. These would be set to black notes, while for words like 'day', 'pale', 'open', unfilled 'white' notes were preferred. At this time, the colour of notes did not necessarily relate to their metrical value.

Staves too, the sets of lines on which notes are written, were bent into curious shapes in the cause of visual expressiveness. One lovelorn rondeau of about 1400 loops its staves into a heart shape. A perpetual canon, like *Summer is icumen in*, known in Latin as a *rota* (wheel), might be inscribed as a complete circle with no beginning and no end, a good indication that such music was aimed at the performers, rather than an audience. Nobody else would know!

Some of John Dowland's sublimely melancholy lute songs, published in the 1600s in arrangements for three voices, have their staves printed at right-angles to each other around three edges of the page, an effect so striking that one is tempted to see another example of *augenmusik*. Perhaps the poet's beloved has him cornered? Or they are at odds in some way. (Ah me! My love and I are at right angles.) The truth is simpler and eminently practical. The three singers can all sit at one table and share the same copy. Cheaper, and very private, but not really eye-music.

By the time of Georg Philipp Telemann, the modern principle of mensural notation was well established. Notes of longer value had white – that is, empty – heads, and could be subdivided many times over. Black-headed – that is, filled-in – notes, were of shorter value, suitable for quick-running passages. Telemann is best remembered for his record-breaking musical fecundity (forty operas, forty-four passions!), and for his embarrassing appointment to the church of St Thomas in Leipzig, in preference to J S Bach. (Luckily for Bach, Telemann withdrew!)

Not many people know his *Gulliver Suite* for two violins, inspired by Swift's satirical *Gulliver's Travels*, first published in

1726, when Telemann was forty-five. Like many baroque suites, it contains a chaconne – a triple-time dance with a recurring chord-sequence – and a gigue. But the chaconne is a *Lilliputian Chaconne*, with a time signature of three demi-semiquavers to the bar, making each bar teem with tiny black notes. The *Brobdingnagian gigue*, on the other hand, moves along in diamond-shaped white notes, strung out in lines like kites in a stiff breeze. And the time signature is twenty-four over one – twenty-four semibreves to the bar! Now, you would go a long way to find a musical bar with only three demi-semiquavers in it (3/32) or one huge enough to accommodate twenty-four semibreves (24/1). Telemann wrote it like that for comic visual effect. The approximation below gives you the idea:

Lilliputian Chaconne

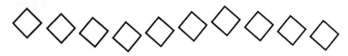

Brobdingnagian gigue

The diminutive Lilliputians dance their chaconne like ants seen through the wrong end of a telescope. The Brobdingnagians, tall as a steeple, Swift tells us, dance a gigue to the improbably large beat of a semibreve, their metabolism as slow as that of Tolkien's lumbering tree-creatures, the Ents. But you would never know, and the music sounds quite normal. All this for the sake of two violinists. Let's hope they enjoyed the joke.

Peter Maxwell Davies, a gifted *enfant terrible* on the English scene in the 1960s, devised a music-theatre piece, graphically depicting the madness of King George III. The text, variously spoken, sung, snarled, fluted, hooted, bellowed and wheezed by the singer playing the part of the king, draws on his actual words, as recorded in the diary of Fanny Burney. One of the king's funny little ways was to try to teach his cage-birds to sing Handel arias. One of the pages in Maxwell Davies's score illustrates this, by writing the staves vertically rather than sideways, then gathering them together at the top to suggest an old-style bird-cage. These sorts of whimsical graphics were much in vogue at the time. In fact, some composers saw graphics as a substitute for hardcore musical information, using them simply as a spur to the creative imagination of the performer. It was not long before the pioneers of the GCSE exam, seeing fresh scope for inclusivity, encouraged music students to do the same, thus offering those with no grasp of conventional musical notation a chance to indulge their artistic bent and salvage a few marks.

Historically, the composer's score has been the sole tangible artefact by which his requirements have been recorded for posterity. That composer will have spent more time – sometimes vastly more time – in the company of his score, than in listening to its live realisation. This original source carried a powerful charge. It is natural that a composer should be tempted to embellish it. The pragmatic Mozart wrote for a fickle Viennese public, often to a tight deadline, but still the score remains paramount, handwritten, practical, and broadly unambiguous. Having joined the Vienna lodge of Freemasons, however, even he allowed a little extra-musical symbolism to creep in.

It is well known that his last opera, *The Magic Flute*, puts Masonic ideas on the stage. No startling secrets are revealed, it seems, and the theory that Mozart met his end at the hands of fellow masons, enraged at his treachery, is fanciful. Wisdom, purity and brotherhood were regular themes in the late eighteenth-century, and to celebrate them in an ancient Egyptian setting, as Mozart does, was about as revolutionary as celebrating apple pie. But Mozart does stress the Masonic number three – three ladies, three spirits, three chords, etc. And since much of the music is in the key of E ♭ , each stave begins with a key signature of three flats. Now, the flat sign in music is not so very different from a miniature trowel (stay with me here!) and the trowel, of course, is a significant symbol in masonry. Freemasonic *augenmusik*, indeed! Who'd have thought it? Certainly not the mediaeval mason who carved his mark into the stone of Rheims cathedral.

A Word in Your Ear

What's the use of singing if we can't understand the words? In Beethoven's *Ninth Symphony* (*The Choral*) the sopranos have to sing so high that the words are impossible to articulate clearly. For the singers, it's like sending a semaphore message from a cliff-top in a gale. One conductor, knowing the difficulty, suggested in rehearsal that they abandon the words at that point and sing 'Ah' instead. It would improve the tone, and no one would notice the difference. Imagine the whoops of delight when an eminent critic, reviewing the performance, made a favourable comment on the clarity of the words. 'Gotcha!' they must have shrieked in tabloid unison.

We know that orchestral players sometimes enjoy making a fool of their conductor – remember the very soft (in fact, non-existent) drum roll approved by Richard Strauss? Critics, a breed once likened to eunuchs in a harem, make an even more gratifying target. The above-mentioned critic's imagination served him well in the familiar finale of Beethoven's Ninth, but where does reality end and imagination begin? In a sense, the deaf Beethoven, conducting the first performance of his *Ninth Symphony*, heard the words better than anyone. For those with normal hearing, detail may need to be sacrificed for the sake of the overall effect.

So when singers sing, what should we expect to hear? Well, in some cases the answer is not very much. In the case of opera, several characters may be singing their various thoughts simultaneously. That's the point. And their voices must carry across a large orchestra to reach the audience, usually some distance away, especially those in the cheap seats! Take a typical quartet:

Girl (soprano): My innocent heart opens like a tender flower.

Mother (mezzo): How well I recall the happy days of my youth.

Lover (tenor): Ah, I will be true to her for all eternity.

Father (bass):   Huh! The two-timing bastard – I'll murder him!

For the listening public, the effort to follow the words can be tiring and detract from an enjoyment of the music. It's tempting to give up and just go with the flow, secretly agreeing with the wag who remarked, 'I don't mind what language opera is sung in, so long as it's one I don't understand.'

But opera is not just music. It's drama as well. So what should we do to ensure we are not missing out on half the experience? Well, assuming the language is indeed one we don't understand, the sensible approach is to prepare the ground beforehand. Go into the opera house with a fair grasp of the story at least. Listen to a recording. Borrow a libretto (the published story laid out like a play) from the library. And these days surtitles (a rolling text) may be projected over the stage, or even on the seat in front as a visual aid. Not ideal, but a huge advance in the democratisation of an art-form often savaged for its elitism.

If an English opera is sung in English, to an English audience, the singers should really be on their mettle. If words don't make it beyond the footlights, it's not the fault of the audience. The composer may be to blame for clumsy word-setting or for scoring the accompaniment too heavily. But the articulation of singers is often the root of the problem. At the risk of treading on fragile operatic egos, companies might provide surtitles even when they're in the language being sung! A visible blow to the artistes' pride, but worth it if standards are raised.

Let's be positive, though. When words and music work well together they reach parts they cannot reach separately. Despite the occasional squabble, it is a marriage made in heaven. As Purcell puts it in the 1690 preface to his music for *Dioclesian*:

> Musick is the exaltation of poetry. Both of them may excel apart, but surely they are most excellent when they are joyn'd, because nothing is then wanting to either of their proportions; for thus they appear like wit and beauty in the same person.

And this monogamous partnership, dating from remote antiquity, remains as strong as ever. Pop charts are dominated by songs rather than instrumental numbers, while the public appetite for good-looking young people singing (very) simple words to (very) simple music shows no sign of fading. Yet to call this partnership of words and music a marriage makes it sound too safe, too comfortable. The seventeenth-century poet Milton saw words and music as sisters. In his poem 'At a Solemn Musick', set to stirring music by the Victorian Sir Hubert Parry, he invoked them thus:

> Blest pair of Sirens, pledges of Heaven's joy,
> Sphere-born harmonious sisters, Voice and Verse,
> Wed your divine sounds and mixt power employ
> Dead things with inbreath'd sense able to pierce…

Sirens not in the air-raid sense, of course, but referring to those mythological females famed for their luring and beguiling tendencies. Milton, the classically educated Christian poet, reaches for good old pagan symbols to add a dash of sexiness.

To call them harmonious sisters implies good behaviour, but sisters can squabble, and words and music can gang up to mug the unsuspecting listener. Sometimes, as in the 'catch' of the Restoration period, they behave like naughty children sniggering at a private joke. The job of the 'catch' was to catch singers out. Taken singly, each voice part is harmless enough, but, in performance, juxtaposed syllables might combine into unexpected double-meanings, preferably indecent. These early prototypes of the 'nudge-nudge' ditties sung by TV's *The Two Ronnies* (Corbett and Barker) were aimed not at the music room, but at the ale-house, where they made a jolly accompaniment to the serious business of drinking. That's if the ale-house singers stayed sober enough to negotiate the three-part counterpoint essential to the joke.

Very occasionally, a pious text may yield an unintentional joke, delighting generations of choirboys. The catalogue listing of Maurice Greene's anthem *The Lord is a light* passed long ago into choir vestry legend as 'The Lord is a light – Greene'. Harmless enough. But pity the prim lady choir-trainer, schooling her charges in the solemn chorus, 'Ah, souls in torment', and wondering why they were gripped with spluttering hysteria.

Usually, when a composer or poet deliberately plants a hidden meaning, the most he expects is a quiet smile of recognition. And hidden meanings will become more hidden with the passing of time. Purcell's great ode, *Come ye Sons of Art, Away*, written to celebrate the thirty-second birthday of Queen Mary, wife of William of Orange, contains a famous duet for two male altos, 'Sound the trumpet'. It begins:

> Sound the trumpet till around
> You make the listening shores resound.

Surprisingly, the two trumpets in the orchestra play nothing at all in this number. But Purcell's two regular trumpeters, John and William Shore, were well known figures on the musical circuit and, as they sat waiting for their next cue, those listening Shores must have been rather flattered by the compliment. In the art-music of the sixteenth and seventeenth centuries, words and music are matched against each other in a predictable, almost naïve manner. Time after time in settings of the Roman Catholic mass, Christ is buried (*sepultus est*) to dark, low-pitched harmonies and rises again (*resurrexit*) to joyous ascending scales. In this way the Creed, a crucial affirmation of faith, was helpfully signposted for those listeners lost in the forest of Latin phrases.

While Monteverdi was in the service of the Duke of Mantua he worked with one eye fixed on the post of *maestro di cappella* (master of the chapel) at the Basilica of St Mark's in Venice, the plum musical job for an ambitious young composer. His elaborate setting of the psalms and hymns comprising the vespers service was really the longest and most impressive unsolicited job application of all time. And despite interviews and tests that would shame the toughest TV reality show, he did land the coveted post. His *Vespers of the Blessed Virgin* (1610), performed and published in Venice, is a treasure-trove of what musicians call 'word-painting', the graphic representation in music of the meaning of the text.

There's a moment when two angels cry out one to another, as angels are wont to do (*Duo Seraphim clamabant*). There are three that bear witness in heaven, they tell us. The Father, the Word, and the Holy Spirit. And these three are one. It's not just the angels that cry out. Any mention of the Holy Trinity also cries out for a touch of musical numerology – and that's what we get. On the words '*tres*' (three) the two solo tenors are joined by a third to make a three-part chord, then on the word '*unum*' (one), the three voices converge on a single note. Three become one. Get it? And in case you missed it the first time they do it again – higher.

Texture – the density of the musical sound – has always been important to composers. Should the harmony just have a few widely spaced notes with lots of 'air' in between them, or should it be tightly packed with many close-set notes? In the *Magnificat*, or song of the Virgin Mary, the rich are usually 'sent empty away' to a conspicuous thinning of the texture, while 'filling the hungry with good things' gets a plump, well-fed sound. And again in *Psalm 113*, when God (according to the King James Bible) 'lifteth the needy out of the dunghill', Monteverdi begins with a low, thick, dark texture, then pointedly clarifies it and raises the pitch. We actually hear some poor wretch being hauled out of the ordure (*de stercore*) and washed down. Rarely does one come across such a tasteful blend of the sacramental and the excremental.

Over a century later, German Protestant composers were at it too. Less flamboyant than Italian Roman Catholics such as Monteverdi, even Bach continued the tradition of word-painting. In his setting of the *Magnificat* – with text in Latin rather than in German as a rare concession to Christmas festivities – the choral writing becomes a controlled hubbub at the words '*omnes, omnes… generationes*'. 'All, all… generations shall call me blessed,' exults the Virgin Mary after receiving from the angel Gabriel the news that she will give birth to the Messiah, and we hear the generations stretching to infinity, chanting like a football crowd. And when she tells us that God hath 'scattered the proud (*dispersit superbos*) in the imagination of their hearts', the words are literally scattered from top to bottom of the choir, voices tumbling over each other in their excitement:

Di–sper–sit	SU–<u>PER</u>–BOS!
Di–sper–sit	SU–<u>PER</u>–BOS!
Di–sper–sit	SU–PER–BOS!
Di–sper–sit	SU–<u>PER</u>–BOS!

One joke became almost de rigueur. With the comforting regularity of the BBC news summary, a psalm would end with the *Gloria*, that neat catch-all paragraph that pays its dues to all members of the Trinity, acting as a final insurance premium before signing off: 'Glory be to the Father, and to the Son and to the Holy Ghost'. Then, emphasising the long-term nature of this glory come the words, 'As it was in the beginning, is now, and ever shall be, world without end, Amen'. And, sure enough, as the choir reaches those words (*sicut erat in principio* is the time-honoured Latin phrase), out come the same notes we heard at the start of the piece. The music here is literally 'as it was in the beginning.' Not a belly-laugh kind of joke, granted, but certainly a quiet inward chuckle as you recognise the allusion. Doesn't that feel good?

In the secular vocal field John Dowland, probably pronounced Dolland, punningly known as 'semper dolens' (always grieving) on account of his melancholy songs, was a consummate word-painter. When a poet mopes with 'groans and sighs', Dowland's finely-crafted music matches him groan for groan and sigh for sigh. Rests break the natural line to represent sobs and gasps. Deep notes on the lute respond to words like 'grief', 'hell' and 'darkness'. Above all, Dowland is master of that languishing cadence affectionately referred to by classical musicians as the 'IVb / V Phrygian imperfect'. Shakespeare is more poetic, but this is surely what he means. 'That strain again', the lovelorn Duke Orsino commands his musicians in *Twelfth Night*, 'it had a dying fall'. A cadence was known as a fall, and nothing falls and dies quite like the IVb / V Phrygian imperfect. Not long after, though, he's changed his mind: 'Enough! No more', sighs the Duke. ''Tis not so sweet now as it was before'. Ah, the frustrations of working for a lovesick employer!

In his poem *L'Allegro*, Milton celebrates the man of happy disposition, as opposed to *Il Penseroso*, the introspective type (like Dowland?), who is inclined to mope. Handel turned these poems into a charming cantata, and in the interests of balance a friend supplied a poetic portrait of the ideal eighteenth-century Enlightenment man, *Il Moderato*. By this time, Elizabethan melancholia had been supplanted by Hanoverian heartiness. Handel's happy man seems inordinately happy. The music paints an allegorical figure of 'Laughter holding both his sides', the chorus seeming to shake with mirth as they sing repeated notes to the words 'La-ha-ha-ha-aughter' and 'Ho-ho-ho-ho-holding'. The sopranos, almost hysterical, repeat their high notes with machine-gun rapidity – 'Lahahahahaha', they titter – while the basses guffaw at a more avuncular rate – 'Ho—Ho—Ho—Ho—'!

As orchestral players honed their skills and instrumental technology progressed, there were tempting opportunities for illustrating poetic texts. Vivaldi's ever-popular *The Four Seasons* is a baroque foretaste of what is essentially a nineteenth-century Romantic concept – programmatic music. This group of four concertos for solo violin, strings and harpsichord is really a colourful meteorological survey of the Italian countryside. In the *Spring* concerto, birds twitter, brooks murmur, shepherds dance to the bagpipes, and a sleepless dog barks over and over again. The part of the irritating dog is played by the violas with a double 'woof-woof' note marked *stroppato* (rasping), an early example of the now ubiquitous viola joke. Need I remind you? Oh, all right then. Question: What are the three most useless things in the world? Answer: A viola solo and the Pope's... Enough! You get the idea.

In the heat-haze of *Summer*, everything wilts, gnats swarm, and the brooding weather breaks into a violent storm. In *Autumn*, harvesters drink too much and then sleep it off, and hunters set off with guns blazing. *Winter* brings a chill to the air, a stamping of feet and a chattering of teeth as we seek the fireside.

And yes, there is a text which tells us all this, though you might not know it. A set of four sonnets, perhaps by Vivaldi himself, provides all the images faithfully represented in the music. In fact, the first edition prints the sonnets as a preface to the score with a letter-code referring to all the relevant features – birds, streams, zephyrs, gnats, dog, guns, and so on. Music doesn't come much more literal than this.

There is Haydn's *Creation*, though. This got off to a good start with the plot already supplied by the book of *Genesis*. That blaze of C major when God declares, 'Let there be light' and 'there was light', stopped the show in its first performance, in 1798, and was encored. With some terra firma in place, and a bit of weather too, the fun begins. The expanded orchestra teems with wildlife. A trilling flute serves as a nightingale, a clarinet rises rhapsodically with the morning lark, and there is some fine cooing from a pair of amorous bassoons. Aware also of the bassoon's comic potential, Haydn can't resist a rudely prominent bottom B♭, its lowest note, as the ground is trodden by heavy beasts. Fortissimo trombones make a splendid lion – cheerful, roaring and tawny, according to the delightfully mangled English version. Strings contribute to this musical bestiary with the frisking leviathan, a 'flexible' tiger, stag, steed, flocks, buzzing insects, and finally the worm, whose theological baggage is weightier in German, where *der Wurm* also means the serpent. The tone is more strait-laced once Adam and Eve have arrived on the scene. The animals behave themselves and eighteenth-century restraint is the order of the day.

Despite the wildlife antics, the singers retain their dignity throughout. This is a sacred work after all. And in the vast majority of vocal and choral music the human voice, that most miraculous and flexible of instruments, has one overriding concern – to combine beauty of tone with expressive clarity and truthfulness. Usually. But things can get thrown off balance.

Words may dominate, as in that lightning-fast operatic plotting known as *secco* (dry) recitative. Think Mozart comedy: 'Wait! I hear my husband! Into the wardrobe quickly! Oh no, there's someone there already! Quick! Behind this chair!' (In Italian, of course.) Things may go further, as with *Sprechgesang*, or speech-song style, where notes begin at the notated pitch, but are linked by a deranged, swooping effect. Think Schoenberg: 'Ah, see how the pale, death-sick moon lies on the black couch of heaven. I think I am going slightly mad…' (In German, of course.)

Words may be spoken in time to music. Consider Edith Sitwell reciting her *Façade* poems to Walton's 1920s music (or the rapper Eminem, according to taste). On rare occasions, the two elements may diverge completely, as in *Sinfonia* (1969), by the Italian Berio, where eight soloists, sounding like guests at a surreal cocktail party, speak disjointed fragments of dialogue over bits of Mahler and other choice musical morsels.

Words may be downgraded to meaningless syllables, as in the improvised scat singing of Ella Fitzgerald, the doowop-showaddywaddy riffs of fifties pop groups, or more recently in Karl Jenkins's pseudo-ethnic hit *Adiemus*. And who remembers those novelty songs of the 1940s and 1950s? Try saying this quickly with a mid-Atlantic drawl, and see how much anyone understands; ah, but that's the joke:

> Mares eat oats and does eat oats and little lambs eat ivy.
> A kid'll eat ivy too – wouldn't you?

Nowadays such a song would carry a health warning about the deleterious effects of ivy-eating.

Words may be abandoned altogether so that the voice, using a single vowel-sound, becomes, in effect, an instrument, as happens in the *Vocalise* of Rachmaninov, or the *Bachianas Brasileiras No. 5* by Villa-Lobos for humming soprano and cellos. Even when no words are being sung, it's still a human voice we are hearing – lips, tongue, larynx, vocal cords – something warm and organic. And how different they sound! The first swoons with Russian nostalgia, the second smoulders with moody Spanish passion.

And we should not forget the oohing and aahing chorus favoured by certain early twentieth-century composers – Ravel in *Daphnis and Chloë*, Vaughan Williams in *Flos Campi* – and done to death in film scores, some of which have now graduated to the bloodless, intergalactic tone-colour of the synthesiser. And hearing those mystical, helium-fuelled voices soar ever higher as the credits roll, we may catch ourselves straining to hear words. Are there any? Or is it just *Aaaah*? Sometimes it's hard to tell, even in Beethoven's *Ninth Symphony*.

Beethoven's Ninth? This – as we used to whisper when cinemas played films back-to-back all day – is where we came in!

Louden Lots!

If performers sometimes have trouble getting the message across to an audience, just how good are composers at conveying their message to performers? Judging by the wide differences of interpretation of the same piece of music, one is tempted to say not very. Just listen to the two recordings of Bach's *Goldberg Variations* by the same Canadian pianist, Glenn Gould. Quite apart from anything else, there are wide differences of tempo. So what is going on here? Doesn't Bach tell us the speed? Didn't he know what he wanted? Well, of course he did, but he probably wasn't expecting his piece to be played by a very idiosyncratic musician, living over 200 years later on the opposite side of the world, using a keyboard instrument he would not even have recognised.

The fact is that most music of the time would have been played by the composer himself, his pupils or his colleagues. Information about speeds, volume, articulation and expression would be conveyed directly by word of mouth. Even in orchestral music, players could be given clear instructions by the composer during rehearsals. The time lapse between the conception of the music and its performance was likely to be very brief. A Bach cantata might be written, rehearsed and performed in the space of a few days, a situation which brings to mind that Hollywood film-music composer who, hassled by an impatient director, is supposed to have snapped back, 'Look! D'you want it good or d'you want it Thursday?' In earlier times, musical employers, often powerful members of the aristocracy or Church, were very demanding. They wanted it good *and* they wanted it Thursday.

Composers in Bach's time would occasionally mark loud, *forte* (f), or soft, *piano* (p), when they wanted deliberate contrast, but before this it was rare. Giovanni Gabrieli's solemn instrumental piece, *Sonata pian' e forte*, from 1597, is possibly the earliest example of a composer marking specific volume changes, and he even brags about it in the title. The time when composers graduated their volume requirements from ppp to fff was far in the future. And even in the late nineteenth century, Verdi's use of pppppp for a passage of extreme quietness in the opera *Otello* must have seemed a little excessive. It's not just those volatile Italians either. In his magisterially gloomy oratorio, *The Dream of Gerontius*, the very English Sir Edward Elgar blends a febrile Catholicism with the eroticism of Richard Wagner, mischievously described by one critic as a mixture of German beer and holy water. In the split-second when Gerontius is allowed one searing glimpse of the Almighty, Elgar marks one brief stabbing chord for the whole orchestra to be played with maximum force. The effect should be like a clap of thunder, but is usually a little disappointing in reality. Was that God? Oh sorry – missed it!

Very low dynamic levels are a feature of the work of the American Morton Feldman, while John Cage went further and reduced one work to total silence. The notorious *4'33"*, written (if one can say that) in 1952 for solo pianist, playing nothing at all for precisely that length of time, demonstrates well the comparative noisiness of silence. Cage's arrangement of his piece for orchestra (yes, really!) involves far more people, but achieves no more silence in the process. If his obsessive quest for silence was doomed to fail, it made a cogent point in the process.

Speed, like volume, is only relative. How loud is loud? How fast is fast? The printing of music started in Italy, and Italian terms for all their vagueness are still much used today. Allegro really means happy, rather than fast. Andante means going along. Moderato means, well, moderate. But how much of a hurry are you in?

At least with speed we can all relate to the familiar ticking of a clock – or we could, in the days when clocks ticked. The clock-work metronome, invented by Maelzel in 1814 as a way of measuring how many beats might fit into a minute, was a sensible idea that got off to a shaky start. Beethoven's early model seems to have behaved erratically. The speed he demands for the *Hammerklavier Piano Sonata (Op. 106)* is superhuman, presumably a mistake. Schumann's metronome markings were radically revised after his death by his rather controlling wife, and editors of his music go for a compromise between the two extremes.

With the advent of electronic metronomes, the old clockwork variety has become charmingly dated, though it was immortalised by the radical Hungarian composer Ligeti in his *Symphonic Poem for 100 Metronomes*. Though a useful guide, the metronome mark should never stand in the way of instinctive musicality, any more than a title. Who would seriously try to scramble through Chopin's *Minute Waltz* in a minute? It's probably not Chopin's title anyway. Any musician, certainly a conductor, ought anyway to have a pretty good inbuilt grasp of the speed at which seconds pass, without recourse to a metronome. Brisk regimental-marching-speed gives you two steps per second for a start. Try whistling *Colonel Bogey*!

Having established a suitable speed and a suitable volume level (for the first note anyhow) one has only dipped a toe into the ocean of interpretation. And here composers vary enormously as to how much guidance they choose to give. Some may cite dance rhythms or national styles as an aid to the player. Minuet-speed or gavotte-speed will mean something even today, though *in the French*, or *German*, or *Italian manner* can be puzzling. At least a dance is likely to have its own definitive tempo, and stay pretty much in time. But what about the Chopin waltzes, many of which beg to be played at brilliantly fast, undanceable, speeds? And how much flexibility are we allowed at expressive moments? The simplistic view of history has everyone trotting out mechanically rhythmical performances up to about 1830, when, in a sort of eureka moment, those dreamy Romantics discovered *tempo rubato* (robbed time), and began lingering here, hurrying there, and generally taking liberties.

Did it really take so long for musicians to start massaging tempos a little? Common sense suggests otherwise. And of course it depends what sort of piece you're playing. The eighteenth-century traveller, musician and diarist Charles Burney (father of the novelist Fanny Burney) had supper with C P E Bach (son of the great J S Bach), and then listened as he played the harpsichord with astonishing freedom and the kind of sweaty passion we associate with much later keyboard lions such as Liszt. One of C P E's party tricks, by the way, was a rapid crossing of hands, until increasing girth ruled it out.

Certainly, with the growth of the Romantic style, composers became extravagant in their directions. *Mit Lebhaftigkeit und durchaus mit Empfindung und Ausdruck*, Beethoven insists at the start of his *Opus 90 Piano Sonata*. 'With animation and always with feeling and expression'. Often preferring their own language to the conventional Italian, German composers ask players to dig ever deeper into their hearts and imaginations with such instructions as *innig* (intimate), *phantastisch* (with fantasy), *zart* (tenderly) – and more than anything *mit sehnsucht* (with that agonised sense of yearning so beloved of Wagner). But the trend was universal. A big rise and fall of volume might be marked within the space of a few notes. A variety of accent signs showed exactly how a note should be attacked. In string music, players were told where the bow must be at any one time – at the point (for delicacy), at the heel (for weight), near the bridge (for brilliance), over the fingerboard (for a veiled tone), and so on.

As orchestras grew larger, movements longer, and changes of tempo more frequent and subtle, the conductor had to be told exactly what was required of the cohort of individuals in his charge. Richard Strauss and Gustav Mahler, both experienced conductors, were meticulous in their directions, urging the tempo on here (without rushing!), broadening out here (without dragging!), sometimes over a long period, sometimes in one dramatic burst.

French composers showed a more elliptical, poetic approach. Debussy's magical piano prelude *Des pas sur la neige* ('footprints in the snow'), requires the music to come 'from the depths of an icy landscape', while many of his pieces ask for a sense of distance, the music borne to us like a fragrance on the evening breeze. Poulenc often asks that the sound be bathed in sustaining pedal, leaving the player to work out the details. But the outright winner in the 'Most Impenetrable French Instructions Class' has to be the eccentric Erik Satie, who routinely litters his scores with remarks in the spirit of the nihilistic art-movement known as Dadaism:

> Open your head
> Don't eat too much

Don't turn over [this when you are still in the middle of a page]
In the corner of the hand
Be visible for a moment
Don't go any higher [in a very high passage]
Like a nightingale with toothache

His titles are equally surreal:

Cold Pieces
Pieces to Run Away From
Pieces in the Shape of a Pear
Really Floppy Preludes for a Dog
Desiccated Embryos
Last-but-one Thoughts

All this is as nothing to the mayhem that was to come. The 1950s, austere in many ways, were a mould-breaking time for the arts. Presuppositions about the very nature of performance began to be challenged by such musical iconoclasts as Cage, Boulez, Stockhausen and Maxwell Davies. But bizarre performing processes often needed lengthy explanations. In his scores for prepared piano, Cage includes a detailed list of 'preparations' to be made before the piece can be practised, let alone performed. We saw in an earlier chapter how Cage's piano was transformed into a new instrument by the insertion of all manner of foreign bodies into the strings. In *Mantra*, Stockhausen prefers to attach electronic ring-modulators, producing a sort of up-market version of *Sparky's Magic Piano*. (Remember him? Probably not.)

In some cases it is the condition of the performer (one can't help wondering if it was chemically enhanced) rather than the instrument that must be prepared. Stockhausen's *Gold Dust* for small ensemble tells the players:

Live completely alone for four days
without food
in complete silence, without much movement
sleep as little as necessary
think as little as possible

after four days, late at night,
without conversation beforehand
play single sounds
WITHOUT THINKING which you are playing
close your eyes
Just listen

Why not try it now? Or later, maybe. When you have a spare four days.

While many composers persisted with tried and trusted methods, others at the cutting edge searched for a new language. Everything was up for grabs. Sections of a piece might be played in any order depending on the whim of the player. Conventional notation (staves, clefs, crotchets, quavers, etc.) might be abandoned altogether in favour of 'graphics' (squiggles and doodlings) intended to convey something to the performer on a subconscious level. Often the visual 'theatre' of the performance was as important as the sounds themselves. Highly-trained musicians could be seen on prestigious London or New York concert platforms, operating short-wave radios, blowing whistles in buckets of water, tooting toy-trumpets, or tracing co-ordinates on maps. Instruments might even be destroyed, predating The Who by several years! John Cage, in some ways the biggest cheese in this multi-coloured cheese-shop, would often call on an ancient Chinese oracle (the *I Ching*, or *Book of Changes*) to dictate the direction a performance might take. Delegation was now the name of the game. Extreme examples invite any number of performers to do anything for any length of time. Composers seemed almost reluctant to compose, with critical musical decisions left in the hands of the player. You get on with it, they seemed to say. I'll see you later!

Such an arrangement presupposes a rapport, not to say trust, between composer and performer. Often composers and their chosen interpreters have worked together for many years, but friendship can take curious forms. If Cage was the big cheese of the 1950s avant-garde, then Joseph Leutgeb was the cheese-king of 1780s Vienna. Music was his main profession – he was a fine horn player – but, like many musicians before and since, he had a sideline. His sideline was a thriving wine and cheese business, set up with the help of money from Mozart's father. A close friend of the composer, Leutgeb was the lucky recipient of four magnificent new horn concertos. But Mozart, with that irritating blend of genius and overgrown schoolboy, showed his affection for Leutgeb in merciless teasing. The manuscripts of the concertos are written in an assortment of coloured inks, and scrawled across the pages are insults directed at that ass, that ox, that buffoon, Joseph Leutgeb. An example of a composer making his feelings very clear indeed.

The Australian pianist and composer Percy Aldridge Grainger, whose jolly *Country Gardens* is his best-known and least interesting piece, knew precisely how he wanted people to play his music and told them so in no uncertain terms – that is, assuming they had a grasp of English. Italian, the language of those decadent Mediterranean types, was anathema to Grainger, who flourished in northern climes, and admired the Saxon and Nordic races. The blond, blue-eyed Grieg was a particular chum with whom he spent much time in Norway, clearing his mind of the sensuous south.

The written instructions in his music are nothing if not eccentric. 'Slow off lots', he tells us. Play the next bit 'lingeringly'. 'Louden lots', he urges where we would expect *molto crescendo*. Once we have well and truly loudened to a *fortissimo* (oops, sorry!) we are to play 'clatteringly', even 'very clatteringly'. A tremolando, the fast alternation of two notes, is a 'woggle'. A tempo indication may be given as 'fast jog-trotting speed', a symptom of Grainger's athletic prowess. His chamber music, a term derived from the Italian *Musica da Camera*, he preferred to call 'Room Music'. His keyboard arrangements are 'rambles' on the 'tune-stuffs' of other composers, 'dished up' for piano. Few chefs can have done so much dishing up as did Grainger. Besides being a professional concert pianist and a keep-fit fanatic, he was a nimble folk-dancer too. Never one to miss an opportunity, he gave his popular *Handel in the Strand* a helpful subtitle: *to be played to, or without, clog dancing*. Thanks for that, Percy.

Quite apart from the rather dotty directions, the stamp of Grainger's personality is on every bar of his music. There can be little doubt that what we are getting is *echt*-Grainger – the real thing. But can we always be so sure? Is the music we hear, and play, always what it purports to be?

The Real Thing?

How often must a well-meaning music teacher have said to a young student, 'Now make sure you get louder here. Mozart puts in a crescendo.' Well, no, actually. The crescendo was probably put in by some Victorian editor who liked his Mozart with plenty of light and shade. And those dusty old editors didn't pull their punches. If a crescendo was not to their taste, you would be roundly rebuked for even thinking of such heresy. In his notes on one of the Beethoven sonatas, Donald Francis Tovey wrote:

> A very silly person inserted a crescendo leading to a fortissimo end. If people still exist who do not see the point of a pianissimo arpeggio without pedal and with an exact final crotchet, why consider their interests?

Why indeed? Flogging would be too good for them!

All of this is no more, and no less, than informed opinion. Whether the composer would agree is a different matter. He might. He might not. For this reason, the professional performer prefers to return to the original unvarnished score of the work, the music as it left the composer's desk – the *Urtext*. It may look a bit bereft of information, but that way we at least have a valid starting point. We know with a degree of certainty that what we have in front of us is the real thing, with nothing added, and nothing taken away. The performer's journey begins from there.

But spare a thought for the listener. Music is, after all, more listened to than read. To the casual listener, technical details may be of little importance, but basic facts should still be clear. Who wrote it? When? Why? For what instrument(s)? Our source of information may range from CD notes (either rather sparse, or very detailed and in several languages), right across to a babbling radio presenter hurrying to the next commercial break. So, are we being given the whole story?

Take a simple example. Gounod's *Ave Maria* was written by Gounod, presumably? Well, only half of it. The tune part, that is. The rippling accompaniment was already there, written as a harpsichord prelude in its own right about 150 years earlier. On to the groundwork of a Bach prelude, Gounod has grafted a new melody. It fits like a glove. A smart move by the Frenchman, then? Indeed. Some may baulk at Bach's ice-cool pattern-making being turned into a penitential wallow, just as a chef might keep his zesty salad well away from rich French sauces. But it is skilfully done, and no animals were harmed in the process. Concert programmes should, and usually do, credit the piece jointly to Bach-Gounod.

It is far more common for the process to happen in reverse; a new accompaniment is added to an existing tune. Printed versions should, however, make it clear that this is merely an arrangement, one person's way of presenting the tune. No such courtesy was extended to the centuries-old folk-song 'Scarborough Fair' when a simple counter-melody and guitar accompaniment was added in the 1960s. On the sheet music and the recording the words 'by Paul Simon and Art Garfunkel' do scant justice to some poor fellow-musician, anonymous and long dead.

There was never any secret about Gounod's Bach transcription, but composers have sometimes been a little more coy about such things. Take the ever-popular *Adagio for Organ and Strings* by Albinoni. Ever-popular, that is, since the 1950s when it was written. But wasn't Albinoni a composer of the Italian baroque, admired by Bach? He certainly was, and died in 1751. Only a few notes of the adagio, a small surviving fragment, are by Albinoni. The rest was constructed by the twentieth-century musicologist, Remo Giazotto. Very lovely it is too, in a rather romanticised pseudo-baroque way. And would anyone be taken in? Certainly, because a) they may not have heard any real Albinoni; b) even if they have, the differences are fairly subtle stylistic ones; c) they are repeatedly told this is Albinoni's adagio; d) they just like it and couldn't care less who wrote it.

Intentionally or not, Remo Giazotto, an academic musicologist, proved it possible to hit the jackpot on the popular classics market. A crafty attacking move by the Italian, there. Oh, and the final trump card? He kept the copyright!

To confuse the public is one thing. To confuse music critics is an altogether different and more worthwhile exercise. The internationally renowned violinist Fritz Kreisler wrote a number of short pieces which he attributed to various baroque composers, in particular Gaetano Pugnani. A fine *Praeludium and Allegro*, still much played, was published as a Kreisler arrangement of a piece by Pugnani. It is in fact all Kreisler's own work, as he later admitted.

Trading on someone else's name has always been a handy ploy. In Mozart's lifetime, people could buy a do-it-yourself kit for composing minuets and trios. No composing skill needed. The job was done by throwing dice, each throw adding a new portion of music from a supply of matching phrases, like drawing Chance cards in a game of Monopoly. A charming diversion for a rainy afternoon in eighteenth-century Vienna. And the creator of this neat novelty item? None other than W A Mozart himself. Well, that's what it said on the packet anyway.

In the minefield of baroque music, there is plenty of scope for genuine misattribution. You may recall the shilly-shallying over the authorship of the so-called *Trumpet Voluntary*. Was it Purcell? Was it Clarke? Was it John Blow? Someone named Blow would have been the happiest choice for a trumpet tune, but it turned out in the end to be a harpsichord march by Jeremiah Clarke. Then there's Bach's most famous organ piece, *Toccata and Fugue in D minor*, now thought by some scholars to be the most famous organ piece by someone else.

And when a piece bears the name Bach we still need to know which Bach. The huge and complex Bach dynasty can cause endless muddles. Peter Schickele, the American musicologist and humorist (how's that for a paradox?), spiced things up by inventing an entirely fictitious baroque composer, P D Q Bach, the point being that his music is so unspeakably awful as to be funny, his plagiarism limited only by incompetence, we are told. It makes sense. A president or prime minister will usually have one cringe-making relative. Why not the world's greatest composer?

Back in the real world, Sebastian Yradier is one of the last composers in any music dictionary, before you get to Zemlinsky and Zimmermann. One of his popular-style tunes won favour with light orchestras some years ago, a tango entitled *La Paloma* (*The Dove*). But he wrote one hit number which will live on. In the opera *Carmen*, the gypsy heroine's first aria is also the work of Yradier. But *Carmen* is by Bizet, I hear you cry. It is, except for that bit. Bizet wrote down the tune, a sultry Cuban *habanera*, thinking it was a folk melody. A genuine mistake, and once the truth was known the printed score gave due credit to Yradier.

Another staple of the Palm-Court repertoire was a waltz song with the English title *Fascination*. Dated 1905, the published score gives the composer as F D Marchetti, but this is a pseudonym (or perhaps we should say nom de plume) for Maurice Ravel, one of the greatest of French musicians – greatest, that is, in all but physical stature. There was a good reason to cover his tracks. In 1905, having failed four times to win the Paris Conservatoire's prestigious *Prix de Rome*, he resolved to give it one last shot. The director of this rigorously academic institution was his old adversary, Theodore Dubois. The last thing Ravel needed at this point was to be known as the writer of sentimental, cabaret-style waltz-songs. But it was to no avail. Once again, despite his status as France's most promising young composer, the prize eluded him. For a while '*L'affaire Ravel*' made headlines. In the aftermath, Dubois resigned his post, replaced by Ravel's own teacher, Gabriel Fauré, whose *Pavane* became a footballing anthem for the 1998 World Cup.

If the broad ocean of music has a 'serious' shore on one side, and a 'popular' one on the other, then there have always been currents and tides pulling in both directions. Eighteenth-century figures like Haydn fished out folksy material from the shallows without compromising the seriousness of their work. Modern purveyors of lightweight pieces have cast their nets into deeper waters, coming up with some prize specimens and filleting them for the mass market. A genteel Andante for organ by Edwin Lemare became *Moonlight and Roses*, crooned by close-harmony groups. The cor anglais solo from Dvorak's *New World Symphony* was sung as *Goin' Home*, while a Chopin study resurfaced as *So Deep is the Night*. The Russian nationalist composer Borodin provided rich pickings: the exile theme from his opera *Prince Igor* gave us *Stranger in Paradise*. *And this is my Beloved* and *Baubles, Bangles and Beads* both came from his second string quartet. And I seem to recall a makeover for the slow movement of Beethoven's *Pathétique Sonata*, sung by the orthodontically-challenged comedian Ken Dodd. Or was that just a bad dream?

Sounds easy enough, doesn't it? A simple scissor-and-paste job. Take a promising classical tune, prise it out of its context, square off the phrases into tidy singable lengths, simplify the harmony, add banal words. Let's try it! What about the lyrical opening theme from the slow movement of Mendelssohn's *Violin Concerto*? Perfect! Put it down into a key which can be huskily emoted by a vocalist with a microphone. Smooth over a few awkward notes. A nudge here, a tweak there, and Bob's your uncle. But what's this? The result seems strangely familiar. Someone got here before us. Yes, it's a song from a well-known musical. I'll leave you to work out which one.

Recycling is all the rage at present. It's always gone on in music and shows no sign of dying out, as pop records rely on 'sampling' from the work of others. Like cooking really. Take one drumbeat, repeat endlessly, add a hint of bass-guitar riff, a seasoning of vocal harmony, one or two rhythmic grunts and wails, and stir well. Like cooking, except that the ingredients don't belong to you. One suspects that, in the end, the most money will be made by lawyers specialising in the new field of intellectual property rights.

No such booty for lawyers in the eighteenth century, when plagiarism was seen as something of a compliment. Charles Avison, a native of Newcastle upon Tyne, was that rare phenomenon, a Geordie composer of the Baroque period. He was also a one-man recycling factory. The concerto grosso, a kind of musical doubles-match in which two bodies of instruments play sometimes as partners and sometimes as opponents, had travelled from Italy (Corelli) to London (Handel) with great success. Publishers were on the lookout for this sort of thing, and there was money to be made. Charles Avison took the easy way out. Many of his concerti grossi began life as harpsichord sonatas by Domenico Scarlatti, an older contemporary. Simply recycling them for strings, Avison enjoyed considerable success, unhampered by any such thing as a copyright law. Scarlatti, their Italian creator living in Madrid, probably knew nothing about it.

But for musical larceny on a grand scale, look no further than Count von Walsegg, a wealthy landowner, aspiring composer and patron of the arts. Walsegg's *Requiem*, first performed in December 1793 at a memorial service for his wife, was quickly hailed as a masterpiece, for the very good reason that Mozart had written it two years earlier, his last major work before his death. Walsegg had dispatched a messenger to the composer, commissioned a requiem and bought his silence with a large fee, a ruse he had tried with other composers. At the performance the Count preened himself, but according to his employee, Anton Herzog, the man who fixed the deal with Mozart and later spilled the beans, everyone knew the truth. Herzog wrote: 'In our presence he always said it was his composition, but as he did so he smiled'. A satisfactory arrangement really – the grieving husband content, his beloved wife honoured, guests enjoying sly nudges and winks, and the composer well paid for his trouble, albeit in this case dead. But that wasn't Walsegg's fault. Rogue he may have been, but he was no murderer. As for the music, Herzog always maintained that no one was fooled. Those guests recognised the real thing when they heard it.

And the Banned Played On

Only weeks before the requiem ruse and his untimely death, the maverick Mozart, still only in his mid-thirties, was busy supervising a production of his new opera, *The Magic Flute*. Beneath its knockabout pantomime humour, we find a celebration of love, brotherhood, wisdom, and suchlike. Nothing wrong with that, you may say. But more specifically the central theme is Freemasonry, a touchy area in the eighteenth century. However innocent Mozart's intentions, it was almost bound to ruffle a few feathers.

Freemasonry – a kind of boys' club for grown men, with trappings of ancient Egyptian mumbo-jumbo – gained a strong foothold during the European Enlightenment as orthodox religion weakened. Mozart and his father were both members, together with Josef Haydn, Emanuel Schikaneder (the librettist of *The Magic Flute*), and Mozart's great friend and possible murderer, Franz Hofdemel (more of that later!).

In view of recurring money troubles and his need to borrow from friends, Freemasonry may have attracted Mozart more as an economic safety net than as a channel for spirituality. At any rate, Freemasons trod a delicate path between a liberal, reforming Emperor on the one hand, and a disapproving Church on the other. Twice in living memory the Vatican had shown its official displeasure. *The Magic Flute* drew no Papal reprimand, but it was hardly necessary. Within weeks of its first production Mozart was a dead composer.

It was not the first time he had courted trouble. An earlier opera, *The Marriage of Figaro* (1786), was based on a play by Beaumarchais, already banned for its subversive message. In it the Count Almaviva intends to have his wicked way with his wife's pretty serving-maid, Suzanna, before she weds. As her rich employer, it is his privilege, his *droit du seigneur*, and nothing must stand in his way – certainly not Figaro, a mere servant. Yet Figaro and Suzanna run him ragged until, bellowing with rage like a child deprived of its toys, he is exposed as a fool and a selfish husband, with the brain and attitudes of a dinosaur. Final score: servants one, aristocrats nil. With revolution in the air, this was not ideal entertainment for the restless lower classes.

Whether or not *The Marriage of Figaro* struck a small spark to the French Revolution is hard to say, but goading a complacent Establishment is an important function of the arts. Two hundred years later, Mark-Antony Turnage's opera *Greek*, an angry modern retelling of the Oedipus myth, might have added the tiniest drop of grease to the skids under the then British Prime Minister, Margaret Thatcher.

While still living in his birthplace of Salzburg, Mozart often crossed swords with his employer, Hieronymus Colloredo, Prince-Archbishop of that city, and wielder of both political and ecclesiastical power. To him, music in church was a tiresome necessity. Forty-five minutes was the decreed maximum for a sung mass. A typical Salzburg mass is a terse, sawn-off affair, while Mozart's luxuriant C minor setting of the same words, the *Great Mass K.427*, belongs to his time in Vienna when he could spread his wings with impunity. Incomplete as it is – several sections are missing – it still lasts about twice as long as its earlier companions.

Mozart and his princely employer just did not hit it off in any way. After many blazing rows in which a certain amount of unchristian abuse was hurled, Colloredo called for the help of his chief chamberlain, whose boot finally propelled the hapless composer out of the room and down the stairs – a shocking example of the Church Militant. No wonder Mozart later wrote, 'I care little about Salzburg [tell that to the Salzburg tourist board!] and nothing at all about the Archbishop. I shit on them both'.

Brushes with the Church began early for Mozart. On a visit to Rome, aged fourteen, he was deeply moved by the *Miserere* (*Psalm 51*) of Gregorio Allegri, a lengthy work with nine independent voice parts, but was dismayed to find the music unavailable, it being the exclusive preserve of the Sistine Chapel. The punishment for a breach of this rule was said to be excommunication. The young Mozart got round the problem by secretly writing the whole thing out from memory after just one hearing (or might it have been two?). That is if we believe his father. Compared with Papa Mozart, those modern fathers who stand on touchlines urging small sons on to sporting triumph are novices. The teenage genius not only escaped the bell, book and candle treatment, but was honoured with the Order of the Golden Spur by Pope Clement XIV, who probably knew nothing about the Allegri business.

Comparatively speaking, the life of a genius in eighteenth-century Vienna was a stroll in the park. Two centuries earlier, with church music the only true measure of a composer's worth, what really mattered, especially in England, was whether you wrote to please the Catholics or the Protestants. Would it be a long, fancy motet in Latin, with florid elongations of each syllable – *Glo-o-o-o-o-ri-aaaaaaah in ex-cel-sis De-e-e-e-oh* – aimed at unaccompanied multi-voiced professional choirs? If so, then the Catholics were happy. The words may not be that clear but, wow, what a ravishing sound! Or would it be a plain, homespun anthem, with the text sung in the everyday language of the congregation, succinct, to the point – Glory to God in the Highest (once only, if you don't mind) – supported by a serviceable organ accompaniment? If so, then the Protestants were happy. How clearly all the words come across, they would murmur – no self-indulgence here!

Composers knew the drill, taking their cue from the Vicar of Bray, that wily cleric who managed to survive the hazardous religious changes of the sixteenth century. Make a last-minute check to see if the person you thought was on the throne is still on it, then set to work accordingly. It may be a matter of life and death. Most set their sails to the prevailing wind, Vicar-of-Bray-style, some went into hiding from time to time, others risked a higher and provocative profile. Some, like William Byrd, could be off-message and get away with it. John Taverner, on the other hand, composer of the *Westerne Wynde Mass* (no, not the modern mystic John Tavener, beloved of Classic FM), is thought to have narrowly avoided incineration at the stake.

Four hundred years down the line and composers in the Soviet Union were finding life equally hard. Now the Church itself was the enemy. Music had to glorify the State. By all means you could write personal, anguished, radical music in your spare time, and keep it in a drawer, but for public consumption something much more accessible was required, preferably called 'Cantata in Praise of the Glorious Workers' Revolution' or something similar. Failure to comply may have meant a late-night visit by men in bulky coats, then sudden disappearance – or at best a new career as a janitor somewhere in Siberia.

Shostakovich played a deadly game with the Soviet authorities, and lived to tell the tale. Few composers can have lurched so giddily in and out of official favour. In 1936, Stalin himself joined in the critical mauling of the opera *Lady Macbeth of Mtsensk*. 'Petit-bourgeois sensationalism' was just one of the charges. Only four years later, his deeply-felt *Piano Quintet* won the coveted Stalin prize. Then in 1948 he was in hot water again, along with Prokoviev and Khachaturian, for writing 'anti-people' music.

But totalitarian bureaucracies are not blessed with much imagination. Bitter, sardonic works found their way into the concert hall with their toes apparently on the party-line. Audiences read between the lines and kept quiet. The open use of Jewish folk-idioms went unchallenged – listen to the passionate ghetto music of the *Piano Trio No. 2*. Poor Dmitri's knuckles would then be rapped again, he would apologise and promise to do better. After the forced withdrawal of the fourth symphony, the fifth bore the heading, 'A Soviet Artist's Creative Reply to Just Criticism'. How often does that happen? A composer, if indeed it was the composer who wrote these words, tells a politician, 'You were right about my last symphony. It was rubbish. I hope you like the next one better!' Sincere or not? What do *you* think?

The Nazi regime was a little more focussed. Wagner good, almost everything else bad. Composers saluted Germany's mythic past, when Teutonic knights kept themselves pure for flaxen-haired maidens, or provided banal marching songs for young people in ludicrous shorts. Jewish composers and performers, dangerously brilliant, were to be rooted out. Jazz, a licentious Negro invention, was right off the menu. Despicable, perverted, cross-dressing cabaret acts were confined to those who could best appreciate them – off-duty SS officers mostly.

In the wake of World War II, banished musicians could return to Germany, though many preferred not to. Some suspected of collaboration were 'de-Nazified'. But in many quarters, Wagner, who died fifty years before Hitler came to power, was still a tainted composer. He still is, especially in parts of the Jewish community. Hardly surprising when you read what he had to say about *The Jews in Music* (the title of one of his infamous essays), criticising them for inherent artistic mediocrity. And his musical rant about German art in *Die Meistersinger* is still rather unpalatable. Despite no official bar, it is no wonder that very few conductors attempt to perform Wagner in Israel.

Now and again, history arranges ironic little paybacks. These days a church marriage, increasingly rare in itself, may mean the bride choosing to come in to the *Eastenders* theme and go out to Abba's 'Dancing Queen'. Once upon a time, wedding music was pretty much non-negotiable: you came in to the *Bridal Chorus* from Wagner's opera *Lohengrin* ('Here Comes the Bride') and you went out ('There Goes the Bride'?) to the march from Mendelssohn's music for *A Midsummer Night's Dream*. How utterly gratifying, then, that for so long Wagner has been forced, in the shape of one of his dreariest tunes, into the company of Mendelssohn, one of the brightest stars in the galaxy of Jewish composers.

And while we are on musical animosities, Benjamin Britten claimed to have played through the piano music of Brahms once a year (what, all of it?) to reassure himself it was really as bad as he thought. If we are all allowed to say a few stupid things in our lives, that would have used up quite a lot of his allowance. His penalty is imprisonment in close alphabetical proximity to Brahms in music dictionaries for the rest of time. Ha! That'll teach him.

Latterly, the Nazi-Jewish question has given way to the Jewish-Palestinian question, a political minefield largely shunned by composers. One exception is the American John Adams, best-known for his opera *Nixon in China*. It reminded us that the disgraced US president Richard Nixon achieved useful things in East-West relations. Audiences nodded sagely. It was history. *The Death of Klinghoffer* did not fare so well. A rather tedious blend of

opera and TV documentary, it dramatised a more recent event –
the murder by Arab terrorists of a disabled American-Jewish
passenger on a cruise ship. The work might have fizzled harm-
lessly into extinction, but there were those who felt it dealt a little
too even-handedly with the issue. Protests and publicity followed
and some of the planned performances were cancelled to avoid
trouble.

Attempts to control the social function and 'quality' of music
are ultimately useless, sometimes tragic, and always ridiculous. In
Nixon in China we meet Mao Tse-tung, chief architect of the
Chinese Cultural Revolution. Remember all those boiler-suited
workers waving their little red books of *The Thoughts of Chairman
Mao*? The opera makes him a rather comic figure. In reality he,
his wife and his henchmen brutally suppressed individual
enterprise. Instrumental soloists, working alone, were potential
counter-revolutionaries. String quartets were banned. Four
people facing inwards might be tempted to plot. New music was
written by committee and revised according to the audience's
stated preferences, a procedure certain to create camel-shaped
works. The composer, temperamentally a lone wolf, became a
lapdog, yapping on command.

But it isn't just politicians, or churchmen, who have tried to
house-train the musical 'awkward squad'. Armchair moralists
have always been keen to join in, with dance a favourite target.
Next time you hear a stately sarabande by Handel, remember that
this slow, courtly dance began life in mediaeval Spain as a lively
youngster, raising eyebrows with its lusty, lecherous motions.
King Philip II lost no time in banning it.

Even the Viennese waltz, with its stiffly whirling couples,
drew censure long before it slowed down into the smooching
shuffle of the modern ballroom. The jive and the jitterbug were
roundly condemned. Despite the lack of bodily contact, their
unbridled physicality was a shock to some.

Recent decades have seen a softening of attitudes. The tango, a
smouldering, hands-on affair, with tantalising flashes of female
leg, is thoroughly assimilated. Arguably the sexiest popular dance
of all time, it migrated from the mean streets of Buenos Aires to
arrive next to keep-fit, sugar-craft and macrame on the syllabus of

your local evening classes. No word from the Church yet, but these days perhaps the vicar has signed up.

With some large-scale musical works it is the risqué dance element that has frightened the horses. In *The Miraculous Mandarin* by Bartok, a prostitute lures men to a squalid apartment, where her accomplices kill and rob them. *Salome* by Richard Strauss has the most famous striptease of all, the *Dance of the Seven Veils*, though it's Salome's death at the end that is truly shocking. At the time, censors were not quite ready for biblical sex and violence on the stage, believing these should stay in the Old Testament where they belong. *Samson and Delilah* by Saint-Saëns – a tale of lust, treachery and extreme hairdressing – had touched a raw nerve some years earlier. There's a time and place for an orgy, it seemed to the French authorities, but not in the theatre.

Saint-Saëns also had the rare distinction of banning his own music. His humorous *Carnival of the Animals* was written for private performance among his friends. Not thinking it worthy of a serious composer, he forbade public performance of the work. It was only after his death that the Swan movement became famous as a vehicle for the dancer Pavlova. As The Dying Swan she drooped and fluttered to the floor, like a sad version of the meringue named in her honour.

However brilliantly descriptive, music is itself morally neutral. The safest place for it must be on a recording. No pictures, no dancing, no exposed flesh, just pure musical sound. But what do we mean by pure? Take Ravel's *Bolero*, for instance. What could be more suggestive? Yet it's still only music. The composer regarded it as primarily an exercise in orchestration, the rhythm inspired by the sound of a mechanical saw!

Words add a whole new slant, of course. They might be elusive – impalpable in the way that faint stars are seen best when you look a little to the side of them – but they burrow into the brain. Try reading Mallarmé's poetic dope-dream *L'après-midi d'un faune*, in English, if you like, then listen to Debussy's orchestral vision of it. Even without Njinsky's choreography, it's pretty sensuous stuff – in a subtle French way, of course. Great art does subtlety well, stroking the imagination.

But for those not ready for the mental gymnasium of great

music, there is always that children's playground of what John Cleese might call 'the Bleeding Obvious' – pop. Commercial clout is the name of the game here, or perhaps its black sheep brother, notoriety, the next best (or worst) thing. It's more difficult these days when, as Cole Porter once remarked, anything goes. But nothing is quite so helpful as a ban.

In the days when the good old BBC served as the guardian of Britain's morals, it was often ready to oblige. How sweetly innocent those murmurings of Jane Birkin and Serge Gainsbourg seem in hindsight – hardly a song, really. *Je t'aime*, they purred breathily in their charming Gallic way, over a musical accompaniment. It was the 1960s and it was duly banned – then everyone wanted a copy. But who listens to it now, I wonder? It was no big deal – the only offending organ on display was probably of the Hammond variety, moaning along in the background. And it's over in about three minutes. Archbishop Colloredo might have loved it.

IV
Finale

Orchestral Manoeuvres in the Dark

The start of the finale might be a good place for a bold restatement of the principal theme. So here goes (fortissimo grandioso): There is more to music than meets the ear. Much more. Much, much more. And that's about it really.

Music is public property as never before. We all know what we think and everyone's opinions are equally valid. Music is a consumer product of immense economic power. Our political masters set the tone. They have given us Britons a Department of Culture, Media and Sport. Says it all, doesn't it? Like everything on the information superhighway, music can be accessed, enjoyed, derided, ignored, tinkered with, customised, deleted, replaced – all at the flick of a finger.

Of course some people still go to live performances, but for the most part we consume music in the dark, from recordings. In the pop video, the sweaty realities of performance are usually airbrushed out to make way for the great god Image. As for classical music, we have little idea how performers look, how they are arranged, how much energy they are expending. Are they bunched together on a concert platform? Are they raked en masse on rostra in a church? Do they cluster in a semicircle around a microphone? Or are they trapped in those individual, transparent booths in a recording studio?

Does it matter? Well, in a way, yes. Musical sound implies movement, and effort, and breathing. Which may be why players of grotesquely amplified instruments feel impelled to respond physically to the power of the sound. Can it be right that a guitar note loud enough to be heard a mile away originates with a twitch of the player's thumb? It helps, therefore, if the rock power-chord comes with a flailing arm or a manic leap. That way the apparent balance between effort and volume is slightly redressed, but still the natural human dimension is distorted.

Stravinsky, never a man for consistency in his views, made

recordings while remaining sceptical of the whole process. The experience of music, he thought, was not about a stylus and a loudspeaker, and grooves in vinyl, but about real performers, visibly breathing and moving and emoting. And he needed to see this. Listening to recorded music is a bit like watching *Ben Hur* on a nine-inch TV, or like the time in the 1950s when top ventriloquists (if you can believe it) exhibited their skills on the wireless.

Musical instruments are so beautiful, aren't they? No wonder artists have painted them almost as often as the human form. Think of the sliced-pear body and fretted soundhole of a lute. Think of the burnished, traction-engine piping of a French horn, the strangely spring-onion-like shape of the cor anglais. The range of varnish on display in the concert hall would alone shame your local DIY superstore – everything from pale, stripped pine to a deep, toffee-apple red.

After a time, we connect the sound of an instrument with its appearance. What a thrilling sense of danger and beauty when the cor anglais player shapes up to begin the long solo in Dvorak's *New World Symphony*! Or, more tersely, but equally fascinating, the three bars – only! – played by that instrument in the same composer's *Symphony No. 8*. Yes, just three bars – about five seconds – in a work lasting thirty-five minutes. A 'blink-and-you'll-miss-it' moment if ever there was one, with the player earning about £5 a note. And who's going to complain? Have you ever tried wringing a note from a cor anglais?

An instrument's voice can be as personal as that of a friend, and as indefinable too. A clarinet sounds like, well, a clarinet. It's like trying to describe the taste of mangoes. Yet with many instruments there's an infinitesimal variation of tone from player to player, and from country to country. It's not so much the nationality of the player, though, as where they studied. Some experts can recognize a Russian bassoon sound, or an American horn quality, and some can even identify an individual performer.

Then you'll discover that when a clarinet and an oboe play the same notes together – listen to the plaintive first theme from Schubert's *Unfinished Symphony* – they make a new instrument entirely. Not an oboe, and not a clarinet, but something else, just as blue and yellow make green. When you look at a painting, the mixing job has already been done. It's over. You've missed it. But watch an orchestra and it happens in front of your ears and your eyes.

Take the curious sea-spray tone of that certain phrase near the start of Debussy's *La Mer*. Drifting out of the murmuring background, we hear a perfect example of orchestral ozone, a cor anglais playing softly in unison with a muted trumpet. A stroke of genius. Inhale that tang! Or more routinely, recall the athleticism of eighteenth-century orchestral violins, partnered every step of the way by oboes. Handel is full of it – listen to the fast fugal section of the overture to *Messiah*. A touch nutty with a dash of lemon, it's the signature sound of baroque music.

And since we're talking nutty, it's well known that a large percentage of the American population believe they have been abducted by aliens. Give them a pencil and they will oblige by drawing their abductors. And here's the odd thing: many of them will draw the English composer John Tavener. Very tall, unsmiling, with flowing garb and long blond tresses – though a little thinner and greyer, latterly – arch-purveyor to the populace of motionless, mystical music, Sir John, as he now is, has always been something of a planetary visitor, even if only metaphorically. But he came in peace and has made rather a good terrestrial career.

And the point is this: he has shown us how high the cello can play. In his platinum-disc-winning work for solo cello and strings, *The Protecting Veil*, the soloist seems to hang for an eternity on the highest notes you can reach on the highest string of the instrument, with the left hand – if you can see it, that is – arched over the far end of the finger board. We might mistake the sound for a violin. This area of pitch is regular violin territory, after all. But where there would be a sense of sweetness and relaxation, the tone here has a searing supernatural quality.

It's a good lesson in listening to string music. The family of strings has a wide area of pitch overlap. Part of the astonishing versatility of a string quartet is that a great many notes, sounding around the middle of the piano, are playable by all four instruments. Knowing this, we become sensitive to the quality of sound we are hearing.

A high cello doesn't sound like a middle-of-the-range violin, though the notes may be the same. Try the Rossini overture *William Tell* – the warm lyrical opening, I mean, not the galloping *Lone Ranger* bit. Sounds like a group of solo strings, I think we'd agree. A string quartet or quintet, we might assume – a mixture of violins, viola, and cello. But we'd assume wrongly. It's a group of identical instruments, five solo cellos, in fact, as we would realise if we were lucky enough to be watching a performance, rather than listening – in the dark, as it were – to a recording. Those five solo cellos, gleaming under the stage lights, are the vanguard in a section of about twelve ranged on the conductor's right. Even on TV, with the sound turned down, the wonderfully poised, balletic quality of cello-playing is evident.

In the celebrated *Bolero* of Ravel, we hear one 'instrument', about seven minutes in, which defies recognition for the simple reason that it's not there! As we reach this point in the perform-ance we may vaguely wonder, is it a saxophone? But we had one earlier in the piece and it sounded different. A very high bassoon, maybe? No, not wheezy enough. A flugelhorn? Unlikely outside a brass band. So, what can it be?

It is in fact a sort of 'virtual' instrument, a composite of French horn and two piccolos. But here's the clever bit. They are not simply doubling each other – that happens all the time. All three are playing in different keys at once! Any musical note, you may remember, has a set of overtones, that sonic barcode which defines tone-quality. Well, here the horn, playing in the key of C, has its normal overtones artificially reinforced by the piccolos. One traces the path of the second overtone – a twelfth higher, in the key of G – while the other matches the fourth overtone – higher still, in the key of E. Thus the relative strengths of the overtones are adjusted, the sound of the horn is genetically engineered, and a new instrument is created out of thin air! Seeing is believing in this case, but when did you last *see* a performance of Ravel's *Bolero*?

And seeing is not everything. You can hear and watch a piece being played any number of times and things may be happening that you will never know about unless someone explains them to you – 'wonderful things', as Howard Carter gasped when he glimpsed gold in the darkness of Tutankhamen's tomb. They defeat the eye as easily as they defeat the ear.

Take a simple example. Imagine all the first violins playing a single note, let's say C, very quickly reiterated while all the second violins are doing the same thing on a lower note (say A):

First violins: C C C C C C C C C C C C C C C C C C C C

Second violins: A A A A A A A A A A A A A A A A A A A A

This will produce a two-note chord with a sustained shimmer to it. The harmony doesn't change, but has a sort of internal energy, like a car standing still with the engine running.

Now imagine a similar situation, but with the notes shared alternately between first and second violins, like this:

First violins: C A C A C A C A C A C A C A C A C A C A

Second violins: A C A C A C A C A C A C A C A C A C A C

First violins will be making a pitch-shape of this kind:

Seconds will make an opposing shape with the same two pitches:

The notes coming out will be the same as in the first example, but there will be an audible suspicion – just – of the violinists' fingers moving from one note to another and back again, very quickly. Once again we hear a shimmer, but a different sort of shimmer. A Bentley rather than a Rolls-Royce, perhaps. For composers this kind of recondite choice is the stuff of orchestration. They care about such differences, and the score will make it clear which effect is required. Listen to the magical first bars of the Sibelius

Violin Concerto, before the violin comes in. Which sort of shimmer is it, do you think?

Such things are not always mysterious or atmospheric. Mozart weaves a more elaborate version of this interlocking pattern in his *Serenade for Thirteen Wind Instruments* (really for twelve wind instruments and a double bass). Quite suddenly, towards the end of the sixth of its seven movements, two clarinets and two horns combine to produce a curious gurgling noise. And with the original eighteenth-century instruments – basset horns rather than modern clarinets, and natural hand-horns instead of valve horns – the passage sounds even more like a melodious malfunction of the plumbing. Ingenious and funny at the same time. Track it down! Enjoy!

Stitching and Stretching

As the last tragic movement of Tchaikovsky's last tragic symphony, the *Pathétique*, begins, showcasing the string section of the
orchestra, an extraordinary thing happens. The six sobbing notes
of a slow, falling phrase – melancholy even by Tchaikovsky's
standards – are distributed alternately between first and second
violins. The phrase itself appears to fall smoothly, one step at a
time, but in reality each part ducks up and down, in and out of
the other – tune-note, harmony-note, tune-note, harmony-note,
and so on. What's more, the violas and cellos behave in the same
odd way. Taking all four parts together, we seem to hear a
smoothly moving four-part harmony, when the players are in fact
weaving an energetic zigzag stitch inside the texture. You can ask
any of the four string parts to play on their own, but you won't
hear the melody from any of them. It only exists as a by-product
of the composite motion:

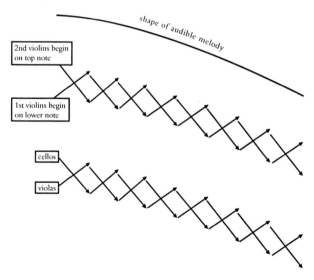

As if to draw attention to this idiosyncratic layout, later in the movement Tchaikovsky scores the same music in the conventional way, the four string parts moving roughly parallel to one another. Ah, but can you hear the difference?

As we saw in an earlier chapter, hearing more than one sound at a time is a challenge to the human brain, whether or not the brain belongs to a musician. At least in the case of contrapuntal music, the various parts are equally melodic and make an equal claim on our attention. Try the rollicking finale to Britten's *Young Person's Guide to the Orchestra*. We hear the perky fugue subject clearly enough from a solo piccolo a few minutes from the end, then, as we are engulfed by a maelstrom of orchestral sound, the Purcell tune which kick-started the whole work rises leviathan-like in the trombones, and the two elements – scampering woodwind and solemn brass – race towards the chequered flag in a thrilling partnership. Strongly opposed in terms of pitch, tone, tempo, rhythm, miraculously they fit together. And we hear it happen!

It's not usually that easy. With practice you might train yourself to hear the three tunes that combine in the middle of Wagner's Prelude to *Die Meistersinger*. Extreme cases like the finale of Mozart's *Symphony No. 41 (Jupiter)* defy conscious aural perception. Here no less than five musical fragments combine, but they are so brief, and dart about so quickly, that we might as well be trying to focus on a swarm of fish. It shouldn't stop us trying, though, should it? And knowing is the first step on the road to hearing.

A composer will deceive the ear just as a conjuror deceives the eye. But there may be a good practical reason. Many routine tricks of orchestration serve as practical aids to a good performance. Here's one designed to give wind-players a chance to breathe. We seem to hear a series of loud, fast repeated notes played without a break:

★ ★ ★ ★ ★ ★ ★ ★ ★ ★ ★ ★ ★ ★ ★ ★ ★ ★ ★

They go on for so long we start to wonder: how do they breathe? Prokoviev is good at this. Listen to the chattering high woodwind in the finale of his *Classical Symphony*. So how is it done? The answer's simple. What's really happening is that players (or groups of players) are working together in shifts something like this:

First flute: ★★★ ★★★ ★★★ ★★★
Second flute: ★★★ ★★★ ★★★

Music plays tricks with time, and time plays tricks with memory. When looking at a painting our eyes can rove across it at will, coming back again and again to refresh the memory over some detail, gradually acquiring a grasp of the whole. A piece of music unfolds inexorably at its own pace. There's no going back until it has said what it wants to say. Our greatest stumbling block to understanding is the imperfection of human memory.

Works using variation technique make a convenient practice ground for listeners. Rather like tracing family trees, though, family resemblances diminish as we move farther away from the point of origin. It helps if the theme is simple and familiar, but composers may stretch resemblances to breaking point as the work progresses. Stalwarts like Handel's *Harmonious Blacksmith Variations* or Schubert's *Trout Quintet* (fourth movement) are a good place to start.

Sometimes the going gets tough. What, for instance, can the connection possibly be between the soulful melody found in the eighteenth variation of Rachmaninov's *Paganini Rhapsody*, and the original jaunty tune of the Paganini violin caprice on which it is based? Once again it's a knowing thing rather than a listening thing. Reading from left to right, the melodic kernel of the caprice tune has a shape something like this:

That little shape occurs over and over again in various forms. By the time we arrive at Variation 18, though, a really swooning romantic moment, the theme has slowed right down, had its key changed from minor to major, and has turned upside down. That is to say, where the original went up, the new version goes down by the same amount, and vice versa, thus:

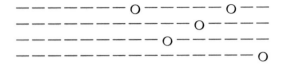

Seen as patterns on a page they are clear mirror images of one another. But our ears are less attuned to registering ups and downs than our eyes. And, heard as music, the moment passes in two or three seconds, quickly overlaid by other more pressing matters.

At least with variations on a theme, the title alerts us to the sort of processes we should expect. Let's finish with a musical relationship so unexpected, so ingenious, you would never suspect it was there. Yet it's easily understood and not that hard to hear, once you know about it. I'd hazard a guess that plenty of orchestral musicians have played the piece for years without knowing what is really going on. It's *Symphony No. 1* by Elgar, that glorious monument to the Edwardian age, brimming with surface confidence and seething with inner turmoil.

Listen to the opening of the second movement, a quicksilver scherzo, then compare it to the solemn *Nimrod*-like theme of the elegy which follows. Totally different, aren't they? Well yes, except for the notes! The first fifty-six notes (pitches) in the violin part are virtually the same in both cases. One takes about five seconds to play, the other has been s-t-r-e-t-c-h-e-d out to over a minute's playing time. It's as if the second movement ends with a winning goal and we are then treated to an extremely slow replay of what has just happened. To work this trick, and make both pieces utterly convincing in their own right, is not bad for a self-taught composer, I reckon.

Stretching is a common enough process in a Bach fugue, where the theme gets played twice as slowly, usually near the end. The fancy word is augmentation. In mediaeval vocal music, too, what was once a traditional plainsong chant can be drawn out to absurd lengths, the singers presumably working in relays as they run out of breath in turn. Meanwhile, the other parts operate in real time, weaving around the elongated notes of the chant like ivy round a column.

Slow-motion video replays lay far in the future for the Edwardian football fan, but it didn't stop England's greatest composer from cheering on his local team. Sir Edward Elgar a soccer fan? Certainly – and it was Wolverhampton Wanderers, since you ask. Aren't you glad to know that?

Frank Zappa, of Mothers of Invention fame, said that talking about music is like dancing about architecture. He meant that it was pointless, meaningless, a contradiction in terms. But to talk (and read) about music is to discover fascinating things hidden away in all the stitching and stretching and bending of the fabric. We see the detail, the weave, close-up – just as Michelangelo on his ladder would have been on more intimate terms with the painted ceiling of the Sistine Chapel than the earthbound tourist. So you are wrong, Mr Zappa. It's not like dancing about architecture. It's more like – well, more like trampolining in the Vatican.

Notes from the Edge

Pavarotti going for the big finish, Mozart's *Queen of the Night*, a Paul Robeson spiritual, Benny Goodman's clarinet at full stretch, Russian Orthodox liturgy, an organist's Amen with the thirty-two foot stop drawn. What do all these have in common? Highs and lows, that's what – extremes of pitch.

We see and hear the world through an arrow-slit of perception. Our visible spectrum of coloured light disappears on one side into the ultraviolet, on the other to the infrared. Our aural range is not much more than a piano keyboard. Pitch your music a bit higher and it might only give pleasure to a passing bat or sheep dog, lower and your only audience might be a wandering whale.

For the musical and non-musical human alike, a healthy ear has much the same range – that is, until deafness starts erasing the upper frequencies. Pity poor Beethoven in this regard. His 1802 will-cum-suicide-note – a real note from the edge – written in the spa-town of Heiligenstadt, near Vienna, bitterly laments his loss of hearing. Bad enough for anyone to find the birds falling silent, or the sound of a flute becoming muffled, but for a musician... and one in his early thirties too. For a time he was inconsolable, but rallied to create some of his most sublime works. And yes, of course a composer can carry on composing even when profoundly deaf, as Beethoven was in his last decade. Denied the joy of hearing his work, he still understood how sounds fit together. But even a genius is human. Even in Beethoven there are moments when, given back his hearing, he might have made the odd revision.

In discussing pitch, we must distinguish between absolute extremities – the high and low points beyond which the human ear stops registering sounds – and personal extremities, if you'll forgive the expression – the highest and lowest sounds that can be sung, or played, by a particular individual. The latter depends on all kinds of variables like physique, confidence, skill, experience, mood, the size of the fee. Circumstances too. Many a shy male will let loose on karaoke night when plied with drinks. Or stand someone on the terraces with a few thousand other football fans, and you'll hear notes being cranked to operatic levels:

> You'll ne—ver—walk—a—lone!
> YOU'LL–N-E-E-E-E-E-E-E-V-E-E-E-E-E-E-R WALK ALONE!

High notes need carry no inherent risk. On a keyboard they are as easy to play as any other note. On a stringed instrument there may be an increased sense of tension, literally, as the player's finger presses on a shorter, tauter length of gut or nylon. Where blowing or lung-power is involved, though, an element of raw physicality creeps in, and with it a buzz of danger and excitement. Can the screeching jazz trumpeter, eyes squeezed shut, reach that final, treading-on-the-cat's-tail note? And he does – he does! We knew he would because it's a recording, but strangely the horror of failure lingers.

Among the most visceral of all musical extremities is the highest note of the highest types of human voice. But does a note need to be that high? After all, high notes are not more intrinsically beautiful than lower ones, and are sometimes rather less so. More than likely the music is attempting to match some emotional peak in the drama. Carl Orff's cantata *Carmina Burana*, a 1930s oddity ransacked by film composers whenever diabolical things are afoot, saves up its scariest moment for the solo soprano. Towards its rackety end, the music skids to a halt and there is silence, a question mark seeming to hang in the air. Will she or won't she? And yes, after all that coy flirting, egged on by a voyeuristic chorus, she finally yields. 'I give myself utterly to you,' she coos, in Latin, to her lover, totally unaccompanied, with an ecstatic phrase that falls like an autumn leaf from a very high, very soft D. Gorgeous, if her nerve holds. The velvety chord that cushions her fall barely conceals a sigh of pleasure from the gentlemen of the chorus.

Female vocal altitude in particular may carry a neurotic or even supernatural charge. Dame Joan Sutherland gave a new lease of life to Donizetti's Scottish opera, *Lucia di Lammermoor*, in which the heroine goes mad with a display of vocal coloratura. A solo flute follows her about in sympathy, the two moving together in a manner suggesting not so much madness as perfect self-control. But it's the high pitch of the whole operation that is crucial here. This singer is literally on the edge, if not already over it.

In Mozart's *The Magic Flute*, the sinister Queen of the Night makes a similarly stunning pitch. Here the message is not madness, but evil. Anyone inhabiting such a superhuman zone must, we are led to believe, have magic powers. And, not to be outdone, a more recent operatic treatment of Shakespeare's *The Tempest* by the English composer Thomas Adès has the spirit Ariel inhabiting even more rarified regions. Here are soprano notes so uniformly high that the text is reduced to a series of squeaks, and the airy spirit of the magic isle becomes a helium-charged Minnie Mouse.

A more gently comical exploration of extreme vocal range occurs in Oliver Knussen's enchanting song-cycle for soprano and chamber ensemble, *The Songs and Hums of Winnie-the-Pooh*. Here Pooh Bear climbs a tree in search of honey, and the whole slow process is brilliantly depicted by the single word 'climbing', sung over and over again by the solo soprano, higher and higher, till she reaches a note of such jaw-dropping altitude that it seems scarcely human. Then we realise it's not. Her very last note has blended seamlessly into the sound of a piccolo. Though Knussen's crystal-sharp instrumentation is more redolent of Ravel's world of mechanical toys than of the English nursery, Pooh's bumpy fall as he is set upon by bees is the cleverest, funniest bit of cartoon scoring you will find anywhere.

At the lower end, the female register tends to suggest voluptuousness. In the male voice, depth means dignity, authority. Bass roles in opera and oratorio are often kings, rulers, priests. Tenors have cornered the market in virility, for with the high male voice must come power as well as sweetness. No faking it at tough moments. What would we think of a Prince Calaf in Puccini's *Turandot* if at the triumphant final *Vincero* ('I shall prevail') in *Nessun Dorma*, he were to float into a semi-falsetto head voice?

Singers in the world of pop and musical theatre do it all the time, but with a bit of judicious microphone-adjustment, a power boost can be delivered. *Nessun dorma* – 'none shall sleep', indeed! Certainly not the mixing-desk operator when an untrained celebrity voice is at work.

It's ironic that the Prince's rousing call to vigilance has become staple fare on the easy-listening shelves. 'Soothe your mood – RELAX!' bellows the presenter on the commercial classical music station. At that rate we will be comatose long before the Prince reaches his final high B. Look in the score of *Turandot*, by the way, and you'll see that *that* note, the high B, is really a very short one, briefly touched on before the voice descends to the final syllable. Puccini writes:

VIN ---------------ce-RO------------------!

Exhibitionist tenor tradition has turned it into:

Vin----C-E-E-E-E-E-E-E-E-—[pose for the cameras]—RO----!

That's opera for you, especially when singers – yes, professional singers, famous singers – learn their parts by rote or from recordings, not from the score. Shocking!

Pitch – fitting letter-names to fixed frequencies – was a slippery concept until 1939 saw the introduction of an international standard, with the oboe tuning A set at 440Hz. In the eighteenth century, pitch was significantly lower, and its trend has generally been upwards. In nineteenth-century Italy, singers needed to know how high the taxing top notes in their score would really be at their next venue. With a top C in Naples not matching a top C in Milan, mutually agreed limits would sometimes be written into their contracts: 'this high and no higher!'

The lighter head-voice or 'floated' note, the tenor's last refuge on a bad day, can also be cultivated as a career option. Those who do so are the counter tenors, starting where everyone else leaves off, but keeping the power-throttle open. There is quite a repertoire for them in French baroque music, where they are known as *haut-contres*. *Carmina Burana* needs just this kind of voice to yowl its way through the roast swan number. More delicate and curiously androgynous is the male alto, a voice-type revived by Alfred Deller. When once approached by a foreign lady in the audience with the words, 'Mr Deller, you are eunuch?' he is supposed to have replied, 'I think, madam, you mean *unique.*' Confusingly to some people the male alto, really a high-class falsettist or upmarket yodeller, is likely to have a deep, bass-baritone speaking voice, and maybe some children too.

English music of the 1600s is natural territory for this voice. In Dowland's intimate lute songs, its wine-glass clarity, its flexibility, and somehow its apparent lack of emotional engagement, perfectly balances the Jacobean texts with their finely-wrought conceits. In eighteenth-century opera too, certain dramatic roles demanded the high male falsetto, but stage performance means carrying-power, and special measures were needed.

Earlier we mentioned personal extremities, and this leads us naturally, or unnaturally, to the castrato. In such cases, 'personal extremities' had been surgically removed in pursuit of a glittering operatic career. A brutally vicarious pursuit by the hapless child's parents, one assumes, or perhaps a wicked uncle. The castrato, you see, could earn stupendous wealth and fame, at least while the fashion lasted. The voice combined prepubescent purity of tone with adult lung-power. And such was the suspension of disbelief that audiences flocked to see their current favourite as the emperor Nero, or Julius Caesar, happily conniving at the bulky, hormonally-disturbed appearance of their hero. Never mind the width, feel the quality, they said. *Plus ça change*, it seems – only now it's probably a pasta-fed tenor.

The range, agility and trumpet-like tone of the castrato voice thrilled composers and audiences alike, while its astronomical earning-power drew curmudgeonly letters to the press. Earning more than the prime minister? Scandalous! The most famous castrato of all, Farinelli, sang in the service of Philip V of Spain for a salary of 50,000 francs a year. So, you see, now it's footballers, then it was castrati. *Plus ça change* (again).

Wagner even considered making the evil magician, Klingsor, in *Parsifal*, a castrato. In the grail legend, Klingsor, once a devout Knight of the Holy Grail, goes over to the dark side, having rejected love in an act of self-mutilation. Perfect casting, you might think. But, by the late nineteenth century, tastes had changed and castrati were thin on the ground. In the end he went for a bass voice.

In *The Magic Flute* low notes are for high priests. The higher the priest the lower the notes. The deep bass voice of Sarastro represents in every way the opposite polarity from the vocal histrionics of the Queen of the Night. Deep means serious, dependable, wise. There are exceptions, of course. In the finest of Britten's operas, *Billy Budd*, the sadistic master-at-arms, Claggart – the name says it all! – spends much of his time growling at the bottom end of the bass stave. But the priestly nature of the deep male singing voice, the Sarastro type, is typically found in the Russian Orthodox liturgy. Perhaps your local choir has had a go at Rachmaninov's setting of the *Vespers*, but let's hope they checked out the bass part first. Some believe that depths like those are best plumbed by singers with Slavic cheekbones, affording specially resonant facial cavities. Long black beards might help too. For the men, I mean.

So, how deep is deep? It's surprising to find how short a distance we need go below the end of the piano keyboard before notes vibrate so slowly that we feel them rather than hear them. Anyone who has stood in a cathedral when the organist plays a bottom C on the pedal board with the thirty-two foot stop drawn can vouch for this. A few organs have a sixty-four foot stop too, sometimes with a warning not to leave it on too long. Reverberations that slow and deep can damage valuable stained glass. And sufficiently amplified – quite a lot – they would turn into weapons, pulverising the organist's internal organs. If a Catholic priest were officiating at the time they would truly be 'weapons of Mass destruction'.

And while we're on low frequencies, let's take things to an extremity of silliness. You know how much physicists love a black hole, one of those collapsed stars with gravity so strong not even light can escape? It's their latest toy. Well – joy of joys! – they recently identified a black hole that sings. If you imagine going a bit below the deep organ note we can only feel, to one vibrating at about 10 Hz, i.e. ten cycles per second, then we can presume there are lower notes oscillating once a second, once a minute, or even once an hour, once a day, once a year. Steady on now, this is getting ridiculous! But no – scientists tell us, so it must be true, that their black hole is singing a low B-flat, though low is hardly the word, lying fifty-seven octaves below middle C, and vibrating once every – brace yourself – ten million years.

Perhaps there are beings, inconceivable, science-fictional entities, who can hear this kind of frequency. They might even have some sort of music. If so, just think how long their concerts must last. The universe might end before you reach the interval. And as for their karaoke nights – it just doesn't bear thinking about.

Unexpected Endings

We all know what a typical composer does, don't we? Apart from write music, I mean. After a prodigious childhood as a spoilt brat, he, for it's invariably a he, falls for a time into obscurity – who wants an overgrown prodigy? – then emerges butterfly-like from this cocoon as a concert-pianist-cum-matinee-idol, flaunting his long hair and Byronic cheekbones, performing keyboard pyro-technics while simultaneously ogling the countess in the royal box. The affair goes nowhere – he is from the wrong side of the tracks, of course – and, retiring in despair to a squalid garret, he pens his final masterpiece before expiring prematurely from consumption, or syphilis, or both. After a suitable period of neglect, the world hails him as a genius.

Such is the standard career-path of the composer, according, that is, to the world of the romantic novelist or the Hollywood scriptwriter. The reality is rather different, but no less interesting.

To start with, creative talent is normally hard-won over a long period. Childhood achievements in music and mathematics, the two disciplines most fruitful in this regard, are outshone in maturity. Even Mendelssohn, arguably the most gifted musical child ever, waited till the age of sixteen to produce his first truly immortal works.

Next, only a select few have had the breadth of talent and the single-minded dedication needed to be a professional composer and a solo performer. We do not expect dramatists to moonlight as actors, though they might. Those superstars among composer-pianists, Liszt and Rachmaninov, did manage to juggle two careers, and even threw in a bit of conducting as well, but many fine composers have hesitated to display their somewhat limited performing talents. One of the most visionary, Berlioz, had only modest skills on the flute and guitar, having spent his formative years as a medical student. And he was not alone in coming to music tangentially from other disciplines. Borodin was an analytical chemist of international repute. Roussel and Rimsky-Korsakov both served in the navy. Handel, Arne, C P E Bach, Schumann, Tchaikovsky, Sibelius and Stravinsky were all marked out for legal careers, before swapping horses in midstream.

Neither do composers, or, indeed, creative types in general, have a monopoly on poverty, neglect, madness or premature death. It might seem so to those who have in their minds a blurred amalgam of the lives of, say, Schubert and Schumann. In just these two cases we find genius, failure, despair, tragedy, disease, lunacy, and a hasty exit from the world. But we needn't look far for examples to shatter the stereotype.

Josef Haydn, born to humble and unmusical parents, rose to be the best-known musical figure in Europe. Still active in his sixties, he was feted wherever he went, his London concert appearances being the hottest ticket in town. Another such composer was Handel, who made more money as a musician than he would have done in the legal career his father had planned for him. Twelve thousand people flocked to Vauxhall Gardens to hear his *Music for the Royal Fireworks*, blocking the traffic on London Bridge for several hours. And that was just the rehearsal!

What about dying young? Of his nine symphonies, Vaughan Williams wrote the last four after the age of seventy, while Verdi, aged nearly eighty, seemed all set to retire before startling the musical world with his last operatic masterpiece, *Falstaff*. Even in the seventeenth century, long before antibiotics and suchlike extended the average life span, some composers just went on and on. Bach's great precursor, Heinrich Schütz, yet another student of law who turned to music, continued composing into old age, and died in his late eighties. As for being neglected and misunderstood, Beethoven himself, everyone's idea of the scorned recluse – dishevelled, angry and deaf – was in fact a colossus in his lifetime, widely revered, and in death was accorded the sort of public funeral usually reserved for generals and statesmen.

The lives of composers are, of course, as varied and unpredictable as anyone else's, and there have been a number of cases where the manner of their deaths can still intrigue and puzzle us. Take Mozart – was he murdered? Suspicions bubbled up soon after his death in 1791, and fingers were pointed towards Salieri, composer to the Imperial Court in Vienna, and still the prime suspect for historical sleuths. Even Mozart thought that the Salieri faction had poisoned him, and he said so to his wife Constanze! The mystery formed the basis of an opera by Rimsky-Korsakov, *Mozart and Salieri*, and has been given a new lease of life by the play and film *Amadeus*, undeniably effective as theatre, yet surprisingly old-fashioned in its depiction of Mozart as the holy fool and Salieri as the embittered mediocrity.

There are others perhaps ahead of Salieri on the list of suspects. Franz Hofdemel, for instance, a young chancery official at the Vienna Law Court. He was a good friend of Mozart's and a fellow Freemason. But did the friendship become strained? Mozart, who had sometimes asked him for a loan, taught the piano to Hofdemel's charming young wife, Magdalena. Constanze tells us, by the way, that her husband was inclined to choose pretty pupils and fall in love with them. On the day of Mozart's funeral, workmen heard a din coming from the Hofdemel apartment and, on breaking down the door, found that Magdalena had been the victim of a horrific attack, her face and upper body slashed with a razor. The assailant was her husband, who lay dead on the floor with his throat cut, the razor still in his hand. Despite being five months pregnant, she and the baby survived. But she was scarred for life, mentally and physically.

The papers had a field day. It's not hard to imagine what today's tabloids would have made of it. 'Was top tunesmith dad to slashed wife's baby?' they might have screamed. And imagine their joy, years later, when that other top tunesmith Salieri 'confessed' to the murder of Mozart. So was he guilty after all? Maybe. But he was in a lunatic asylum at the time and much given to senile ramblings.

Until quite recently, all we knew of Tchaikovsky's death was the sanitised version given by his brother Modeste. Recent evidence points to something more scandalous. Earlier in his life, the neurotic Tchaikovsky, a closet homosexual, had rushed into a disastrous marriage and a nervous breakdown. In his fifties, when he was renowned as Russia's most eminent composer, it seems he was warned by his coterie of law-school friends that someone was on the point of spilling the beans about his liaison with a young, male relative of the Imperial family. He must act. So a few days after the premiere of the *Pathétique Symphony* he took his own life, possibly by poison, and his reputation was saved.

Perhaps we shall never know the truth for certain. But listen again to the opening bars of the finale of this symphony, with its dirge of weaving, sobbing strings. Do you hear it differently now?

The Polish pianist and composer André Tchaikovsky – no relation to the Russian – made a macabre bid for a posthumous theatrical career by bequeathing his skull to the Royal Shakespeare Company, for use in the graveyard scene in Hamlet. Perhaps a few textual adjustments would be appropriate:

Hamlet: Alas, poor Yorick! I knew him, Horatio. A fellow of infinite jest, of most excellent fancy. Wrote a rather good clarinet sonata too.

Horatio: E'en so, my lord. And have you heard his settings of some of Shakespeare's sonnets?

Hamlet: Can't say I have, Horatio. Sonnets by whom, did you say?

In the musical pantheon of the BBC, Schönberg and his two favourite pupils, Berg and Webern, were revered, at least in the 1960s, as the glorious and undivided Holy Trinity. To arbiters of musical taste Arnold Schoenberg – to give the Americanised spelling of his name – reigned as God the Father Almighty, creator of a new Heaven and Earth. 'Let there be serialism,' he said. And behold, there was serialism, a method of composing where notes line up in a predetermined order, regardless of conventional keys and harmonies. He fled the Nazis, settled in the USA, and died in Los Angeles in 1951, but not before playing a few games of table tennis with a youthful André Previn.

His two pupils predeceased him. Alban Berg, the human face of serialism, developed septicaemia from a mosquito bite four months after completing his sensuous violin concerto of 1935, an elegy to the memory of eighteen-year-old Manon Gropius, beautiful daughter of Mahler's widow by her second marriage.

The music of Anton von Webern, the Holy Ghost of this serial Trinity, inhabits a pure region where the air can be breathed only by the true believer. A supporter of the Nazi regime in Austria, even when they banned his music, he was accidentally shot dead in 1945 by a nervous American sentry rooting out black-marketeers and collaborators.

Here are a few more musical deaths to ponder. Jean-Baptiste Lully, pioneer of French baroque opera and colleague of Molière, would beat time on the floor with a large stick – that is, until he clouted his foot rather hard, developed gangrene, and died. It's the one thing schoolchildren always remember about music of the French baroque era, if they remember anything. Since he was one of the most ruthlessly ambitious characters in musical history, the incident may have engendered a certain amount of behind-the-hand sniggering at the French court.

In 1916, the liner Sussex was sunk in the English Channel by a German U-boat. Among the many drowned was the Spanish pianist-composer, Enrique Granados, a rare case of a musical career cut short by a torpedo. In 1930, Philip Heseltine, who called himself Peter Warlock and dabbled in black magic, was found dead in a gas-filled room. Despite the jury's open verdict, his heavy mood-swings and drink habit suggest suicide.

In all spheres of human endeavour, we meet the tragedy of unfulfilled promise. War, disease and accidents take their toll, but in the musical world premature death is thrown into sharper focus by youthful precocity. In English music alone, we find the brilliant violinist and composer Thomas Linley, friend of Mozart, who died at the age of twenty-two in a boating accident. Military casualties include the viol player and theatre composer William Lawes, killed fighting in the Royalist army at the siege of Chester.

In World War I, the gifted George Butterworth, remembered for his orchestral idyll *The Banks of Green Willow*, died in action at the battle of the Somme, aged thirty-one. The more classical elegance of William Denis Browne's *To Gratiana Dancing and Singing* stands as an epitaph to his soldier's death in Turkey, aged twenty-seven. Ivor Gurney, composer and poet, survived gassing at Passchendaele only to descend into madness. Listen, dry-eyed if you can, to the homesickness of his song 'Severn Meadows', written in the trenches:

Only the wanderer
Knows England's graces,
Or can anew see clear
Familiar faces.

And who loves Joy as he
That dwells in shadows?
Do not forget me quite,
O Severn meadows.

It's that 'quite' which is so heartbreaking, isn't it?

Apart from World War I casualty William Denis Browne, and English Civil War victim William Lawes, another composer and bearer of the apparently unlucky name of William was the Londoner William Hurlstone. A pupil of Charles Stanford (like so many of his generation) he succumbed in 1906 to bronchial asthma at the age of thirty. Clarinetists would be the poorer without his *Four Characteristic Pieces*. Then there was the promising, but frail, young Yorkshireman, William Baines. Sparkling new piano works tumbled from his pen, but his twenty-third birthday proved to be his last.

What might they have achieved? Great things? Or might they have settled into a rut of middle age and mediocrity? Who knows? But let's pay tribute to them – preferably to the accompaniment of Schubert's String Quintet, written shortly before his syphilitic death at the age of thirty-one – as they take their places in the glorious host of might-have-beens, musicians in that dim, never-ending, endlessly fascinating concert of unheard melodies.

A Graceful Exit

It's so important for things to end in the right place, isn't it? Take an example:

> There was a young man of Rangoon
> Who wrote a brief song to the moon.
> It sounded just fine
> Till the very last line
> Which ended a bit soon.

Something wrong, I think you'll agree. So how about this?

> There was a young man of Hong Kong
> Who set about writing a song.
> It started quite well
> But he just couldn't tell
> Why the last bit sounded ever so slightly wrong.

Not much better, is it? One ends too early, one too late. Things really do have to stop when they are supposed to stop.

The famous dancer and choreographer Robert Helpmann once summarised the problem of dancing naked. 'Not everything stops when the music stops,' he said. Well, there's a similar problem with some music. It reaches its natural end, but the composer goes on.

'That Beethoven, eh? Doesn't know where to stop, that's his trouble.' How often have you heard that kind of comment, especially in relation to the *Fifth Symphony*? And to be fair, the final bars can seem rather ridiculously prolonged. A bit like a temper tantrum, or a shouting match with both sides set on having the last word. '*Au contraire*,' opine the initiated, 'not a note too many. The effect is uplifting, magisterial, transcendent,' and all those other Sunday broadsheet terms as well. Beethoven knew what he was doing. If it doesn't work, blame the conductor.

Some composers know exactly when and how to stop, and get it right first time. Others may have second thoughts, prompted by comments from friends or publishers, or by the reality of live performance. An ending that seems fine on the page may be too abrupt when heard in real time. Bartok's *Concerto for Orchestra* and Elgar's *Enigma Variations* are cases in point, both having had their endings rewritten and extended. Mozart had every confidence in his own judgement. Blessed with an instinctive grasp of form, he begged to differ when the Emperor criticised his music for having 'too many notes'. 'Just as many as are needed, Your Majesty,' he insisted.

A work should have its own internal growth, developing logically from a starting point to a natural and satisfying finish. The Parsee composer Shapurji Kaikhosru Sorabji – born in 1892, in Chingford, Essex – would tell you that his piano work *Opus Clavicembalisticum* simply had to unfold over two hours. The fourth of Webern's *Six Orchestral Pieces*, on the other hand, ends quite satisfactorily after only six bars, or about twenty seconds. The one, it seems, could not be any shorter. The other need be no longer. In each case, the process of moving from start to finish is complete. That is how the composer planned it, and we must trust him.

The cut-and-paste approach to modern life can show a rude disregard for this process. In a world that fears silence almost more than anything – witness the frenzied prattling of the radio DJ – music is squeezed out like filler to plug a gap, or is stuck on like a plaster to hide an uncomfortable pause. It may be repeated mindlessly, or truncated in mid-flow. Think of those loops of synthetic pap spewed out behind broadcast traffic reports, or those tinny gobbets of Vivaldi wedged between 'You-are-being-held-in-a-queue' and 'Hello-you're-speaking-to-Kelly-how-may-I-help-you?'

But music can be made to fit, and still make sense. When Tchaikovsky wrote a ballet *pas de deux*, he might well have been required to fill a preset number of bars at a certain tempo. That was his job. Start here. End here. With modern precision timing, film and TV composers can go further, extruding their product to fit a scene with split-second accuracy. That is *their* job. But large works, with their own internal logic, may be dismembered for easier public consumption. And when music is spooned out in digestible dollops, can we be sure we are seeing the bigger picture, hearing the real beginning, the real end?

English hymn books introduced a whole generation to twenty-four bars from Holst's orchestral suite *The Planets*. Those twenty-four bars happened to fit Cecil Spring Rice's poem 'I Vow to Thee, My Country'. But listen to the whole *Jupiter* movement, and marvel at how the first three very quick notes are pulled, and stretched and tossed about till they become the opening of that rather slow tune. Remember too that this twenty-four-bar tune is only the middle section of *Jupiter*, and that *Jupiter* itself is only the central movement of seven, which, when played in full, last for fifty minutes.

Millions who had never heard the massive symphonic poem *Also Sprach Zarathustra* by Richard Strauss were bowled over by the first couple of minutes of it in the film *2001: A Space Odyssey*. TV has given us hunks from Orff's *Carmina Burana* in an after-shave ad, from Katachurian's ballet *Spartacus* in a maritime drama series, and, in 1984, we had repeated airings of just the final part of Ravel's sixteen-minute-long *Bolero* in an Olympic ice-dance routine. Taxed with artistic vandalism, the skaters would, I suppose, slide out of it by pleading competition time constraints.

Some harsh music editing has, of course, been arranged by the Grim Reaper, and history is littered with unfinished works. Mozart's *Requiem* and Puccini's opera *Turandot* are well-known examples, but surely the most dramatic is the *Hejnal Mariacki*, a trumpet fanfare still sounded hourly in the central square in Krakow, Poland. Its abrupt end commemorates a partial performance in the fourteenth century, when the player was shot in mid-blast by a Tartar arrow. Editing could be savage in mediaeval times.

But what about the savage electronic editing we hear nowa-days? Music editors in the time-obsessed world of TV are paid to dissect a pre-existent piece of music, with the casual sadism of a small boy who wonders how well a beetle will walk with only five legs. The musical transplants of the past – selections from this, abridgements of that – have been replaced by a microsurgery whose technical sophistication belies the aesthetic brutality involved.

Whether anyone notices this, let alone cares about it, depends on the seriousness of the offence. What degree of mangling did the music undergo? The listener, assuming he is indeed listening, may not know the way the piece *should* go. And if he doesn't, he may not be affronted by the odd few missing bars. But those with some experience of music, and a sense of its structure, will wince inwardly as opening credits end in an unresolved key – even that banal BBC TV soccer theme can offend – or as a commercial snips a piece out of the introduction to Handel's *Zadok the Priest* (P&O Cruises!). Or as an opening phrase – the pretty bit – is stitched directly to a final cadence, as happened to the aria from Bach's *Goldberg Variations* in a TV trailer for – of all things – a gala Bach Week on BBC Radio 3.

Greek mythology tells us of Procrustes, who used to waylay travellers and tie them to a bed, before setting to work on them. No, it's not what you're thinking. He was more of a chiropractor, really – and obsessively tidy. If his victims were too short for the bed, he stretched them, if too tall, he lopped bits off. They must be made to fit, that's all. A cruel and unusual compulsion, most would agree. Today we'd have a name for it. There'd be support groups. Someone would make a TV documentary, Procrustes murmuring in shadowy anonymity about his terrible childhood.

The modern music editor is a Procrustean figure. Things must fit. It's different for a film or TV soundtrack, of course, where the torture is aesthetic rather than physical. A few seconds here, a few seconds there, and the great god of time limits is placated. Only the fussy old pedants are offended. After all, it's only music.

But good music doesn't want to be longer or shorter. It starts, it says what it needs to say, in its own time, in its own way, and it ends. And composers take great care over endings. Endings are crucial. Triumphant, enigmatic, bombastic, comical, unexpected, they set the seal on the piece. Why not spend a happy afternoon comparing endings? In each case you need to hear the whole thing to judge the full impact. Try a clutch of matching genres. If you have enough time, fifth symphonies are a fruitful area for endings: Beethoven unable to stop whacking that C major chord; Mahler exuberant to the point of hysteria; Sibelius swinging Thor's hammer in a rather dangerous way; and Shostakovich giving his Soviet masters, deaf to irony, the sort of blazing endorsement they craved.

There have been innumerable quiet endings as well, of course. But some composers have gone further, attempting a slow, slow descent into silence, towards that moment when, after a breathless pause – 'is that it?' – we wait for one bold member of the audience to lead the growing ripple of applause – 'trust me, I know this piece!'

Sometimes it can seem – and this is where a private hearing in a darkened room may be preferable – as if the music has not stopped at all, but as if it has just drifted out of earshot on to some higher plane, beyond the reach of human perception. Into this category come the dying bars of Mahler's *Das Lied von der Erde*, an achingly sad farewell to life, and Vaughan Williams's *Sixth Symphony*, as desolate a musical landscape as you will hear.

The effect may be aided by a little crafty stage management. In the final movement – *Neptune* – of Holst's *Planets*, there is a slow oscillation of two chords sung by women's voices. The composer suggested that the choir should be placed in an adjoining room, audible but invisible to the audience. As the orchestra's spectral shimmerings dwindle and cease, when only the voices are left, someone silently and slowly closes the door to the room. A perfect fade to nothing in the days before mixing desks.

A comic finish is a challenge for a composer. And here we should distinguish between the smart, cocky, 'that's your lot' sort of finish, and the kind where the actual process of finishing is being mocked in some way. In one, an offhand musical shrug rounds off a witty romp – Bernstein's overture to *Candide*, maybe. In the other – say, Arnold's *Grand, grand overture* for three vacuum cleaners, floor polisher, four rifles and orchestra – the effect may be plain silly, or funny, according to taste.

Musical clichés have long been a target for mockery. Rossini, after a late career-shift from opera to cooking, returned to composing form with what he called his 'sins of old age'. His tongue-in-cheek *Petite Messe Solennelle* (*Little Solemn Mass*) of 1863, neither little nor especially solemn, pokes affectionate fun at those of his operatic colleagues who just didn't know when to stop.

Mozart's jolly divertimento, *Ein musikalischer Spass* (*A Musical Joke*), can be more embarrassing than funny. His idea was to mock those second-rate composers who got things a bit wrong – staying in one key too long, making impracticable demands on their instruments, mercilessly flogging one tedious rhythm, and so on. The trouble is – perhaps because it's Mozart – none of it is quite bad enough to make us laugh, even if we see the point. And at the end of this rather long shaggy-dog joke comes the punchline. The last three chords are loud, ugly dissonances, which really shock the listener. Our mocked second-rate composer is now totally incompetent, or drunk, and the effect is less a punchline, more a punch in the face!

Haydn's String Quartet in E flat, *Opus 33 No. 2*, known as *The Joke*, is as subtle and charming as the man himself. Written in 1781, this is a rare example of classical music raising a laugh from the audience, or at least a chuckle of appreciation. The perky little theme that forms the basis of the final rondo is played one last time, with a cheeky silence between each phrase. The music continues with the phrases getting shorter and the gaps longer, surely the most remarkable use of measured silences in the classical repertoire. (Not pauses, by the way, as the players are still counting in time.) Just as we think we've got the point – 'ah, this really IS the end' – it isn't. But we won't be caught a second time. We see the pattern now. 'This isn't quite the end – there IS more!' But it is – and there isn't! There's not much to link string quartets with World Cup football, but as that TV commentator once said: 'They think it's all over… It is now!'

We find another extraordinary ending, no laughing matter this time, in the *Symphony No. 45*, known as *The Farewell*. Haydn's employer, Prince Nikolaus Esterhazy, was rather remiss when it came to giving his orchestral players leave to visit their families. So Haydn arranged a musical walkout. The finale is slow, and as it draws to a close the number of players is gradually reduced. In a performance before the prince, each player finished his part, blew out his candle and left the platform, until only two violins remained.

What other symphony ends with only two solo violins? Apparently the hint was taken, and the next day the court returned to Vienna.

Lately, the literary world has seen a vogue for sequels. Writers want to tell us what happened to Jane Eyre after she married Mr Rochester, or whether the second Mrs De Winter fared better than the doomed Rebecca. No harm in that, I suppose. But music, not intrinsically a narrative affair, is closer to architecture than to fiction. You wouldn't add a conservatory to the Parthenon, would you? Sometimes, though, the temptation is too much. The English composer Colin Matthews has written a haunting additional movement, *Pluto the Renewer*, to Holst's *Planets Suite*. The outermost planet of our solar system was discovered a full fourteen years after Holst finished the work. Imagine him in 1930, when he was still alive, reading the news over breakfast: 'Oh God, not another bloody planet. I thought I'd finished.' But the work is astrological-mystical, rather than astronomical-scientific, and he was not inclined to tinker with his original conception. Anything that is unnecessary is bad art, he once said, in a typically uncompromising comment that would wipe out most popular culture at a stroke. And, anyway, it looks as if Pluto may be demoted to an asteroid after all.

What about Haydn, though? He was an Enlightenment man, curious about the natural world. When he visited Bath, he called on the musician-astronomer William Herschel to inspect his new telescope. Might not the genial Haydn appreciate an update on scientific matters? So maybe we should supply an extra chorus at the end of his biblical oratorio, *The Creation*. Let's call it 'Achieved is the glorious process of evolution by natural selection (this far, anyway)'. Then again, it doesn't quite ring true, does it? Music, you see, has a peculiar kind of truth, which is non-negotiable.

How to protect your ending, then? John Cage had a good idea. Despite his reputation as something of a snake-oil salesman, he had many good ideas. Why not define a piece of music exclusively in terms of its duration? You probably remember 4'33". The clue is in the title. It's a segment of silence, or ambient noise perhaps, with the end coming four minutes and thirty-three seconds after the beginning. Not too soft, not too loud, and precisely in the right place. Tinker with that at your peril.

'The Rest is Silence...'
– Hamlet, V.ii

With nothing left to say, we fall silent. Things sink into silence. The route into silence is metaphorically downwards. A heartbeat dances on high ground, tracing out jagged peaks on a screen, until it plummets to the ground level of zero frequencies. When the music stops, we descend from a cliff top of sound, to a sea of silence. This descent is by no means instantaneous – between the two lies a shelving shoreline of resonance – but soon the sound of sound morphs seamlessly into Paul Simon's sound of silence.

Did you enjoy all the sibilants in that last sentence? Try reading it, or hissing it, aloud. That's it. Now you know they're there, and you can relish that, can't you? Like music really. Knowing amplifies hearing.

Silence means different things to different people. Those who meditate are nourished by it. For broadcasters, it is the enemy: 'Now over to Simon in Hong Kong – Hello Simon – Are you there? – Simon?' But silence can be eloquent too, as anyone knows who has stood in a Remembrance Day gathering, or waited long seconds for the Archbishop's answer to a wily radio journalist, who has asked him what he really thinks about the invasion of Iraq.

The rest is silence. Hamlet's dying words have a certain irony when you reflect on the oceans of academic ink spilled in the four centuries of noisy analysis that has been applied to one Danish prince. The troubled Hamlet cries out to be understood, and for that you must *read* the text. Actors have their place, but reading Shakespeare sheds a special kind of light.

A musical score is less accessible, certainly to the non-expert. Help is needed. Can anything be more stubbornly mute than unperformed music? Mute, yet straining to be heard – like those oil paintings of lutes and viols lying amid ripe fruit; like those angelic trumpets in stained glass; not to mention the pagan revellers on Keats's Grecian urn, piping their ditties of no tone.

In our own time, there is the near-miraculous encoding of a Beethoven symphony into binary information on a disc. And spare a thought for those lonely recordings heading for infinity on a Voyager spacecraft, the best humanity has to offer. How long before some extraterrestrial inserts them into an appropriate aperture, pours itself a gin, and lies back to savour the distinction between Glenn Gould's playing of Bach and 'Johnny B Goode' as sung by Chuck Berry? Yes – they're both there, and much else besides!

Pity that poor, puzzled extraterrestrial. But let's hope he/she/it has the alien equivalent of imagination as well as intellect, a taste for mystery as well as information. If we had only sent the London telephone directory, then, with the right key, its function could be grasped. But music…?

What does music mean? Often little, or nothing at all. A train journey has no meaning as such, but you'll enjoy it more if you know what to look out for on the way. Language, both spoken and written, does meaning rather well. It needs to. It's what you'd expect from, say, a notice giving instructions in case of a fire. But playfulness, ambivalence, has its charm too. The 'meat and two veg' of scientific precision may benefit from a spicy side-salad of poetic ambiguity. Take that Grecian urn again. In his ode, Keats addresses it as: 'Thou still unravish'd bride of quietness'.

But is that still as in 'unmoving', or still as in 'so far'? Well it's one or the other – we shall never know – or maybe it's both. That's the richness of language. It teases us, makes us ponder, blink, laugh even. 'I'm skipping as high as I can,' pants the small girl outside the waste disposal depot. Above her a sign reads: Skip Hire.

So it is with music. Framed by silence, and full of holes like a Swiss cheese, it thrives on the equivocal, the enigmatic.

Very broadly speaking, emotional experience happens in the right-hand side of the brain, while the left-hand side deals with the processing of information. The ancient Greeks made the same distinction in their own way. The god Dionysus presided over our basic human instincts – drunkenness an extreme example –

and our higher nature – knowledge, wisdom, the arts – was in the hands of light-bringing Apollo.

Music-making implies performing – playing or singing. But before it can be played or sung, music must literally be made. The musical composition is an artefact, put together by a craftsman with special skills. And finding your way through it may not be easy. The Greeks understood that too. Their archetypal craftsman was Daedalus, a builder, a cunning constructor of things. But what things? Houses? Bridges? Shops? Temples? No, none of these. He was a maker of mazes. That, I think, is as it should be.

Printed in the United Kingdom
by Lightning Source UK Ltd.
126923UK00001B/22-30/A